SCARY FUN!

DISCOVERING THE EXHILARATION OF SHARING YOUR FAITH

TOM ELIE

AUTHOR OF THE **ONE MINUTE WITNESS**

Published in the United States of America by Oasis World Ministries
PO BOX 2244, Maple Grove, MN 55311

ISBN 978-1-943898-00-8 (Paperback edition)

ISBN 978-1-943898-01-5 (E-Book edition)

By jingo he's got it!... If you pick up the book, you can share in the excitement that Tom and I have experienced for well over 30 years and it will continue into eternity.

—**Evangelist William Fay**, Author of *Share Jesus Without Fear*

I am thrilled to endorse Tom Elie's new book… *SCARY FUN!* It will equip and challenge you to **put feet to your faith**. You will find new success in joyfully sharing your own story. You will overcome both the rational and irrational fears that have kept you silent. This will be **a breakthrough book for you!**

—**James O. Davis**, Cofounder Billion Soul Network,
Founder Cutting Edge International

SCARY FUN! **is challenging** and invitingly practical. How many more people might come to Christ if we simply spoke up more often? In this immensely helpful book, **Tom Elie disarms our fears** and provides us with an easy, non-manipulative approach to starting spiritual conversations with people. Tom's personal honesty regarding his own journey only adds to the engaging quality of this wonderful book.

—**James Bradford**, General Secretary of the Assemblies of God

The reason my wife and I started River Valley Church 18 years ago was simple: to reach lost people. I believe this is a requirement of all Christians, regardless of positions or giftings. In his book, *SCARY FUN!*, Evangelist Tom Elie **teaches us how to address the fear** that can come with sharing our faith and to "do it afraid". His practical resources, experienced tips and exciting stories will have any believer energized to **get out there and reach those not yet here!** Let's reach more people!

—**Pastor Rob Ketterling**, River Valley Church,
Author of *Change Before You Have To*

Tom Elie is a Statesman, a Pastor, a Missionary, and a friend, but most of all he is an Evangelist! **His passion for souls is contagious!** Tom's insight of making witnessing a part of your daily living is **refreshing and liberating**. You will be activated in your life as you digest *SCARY FUN!*

> —**Rev. Dominic Galati, Jr.**, Founder and President
> Compelled 2 Go Impact Int'l

Someone said "The saved and the unsaved have one thing in common: they're both uncomfortable with evangelism". Tom Elie's book *SCARY FUN!* changes that for both groups! This book should be **required reading** for every Bible College student and every serious Christian. We should hold each other accountable to practice it's truths. This compilation of **helpful tools, tips and strategies** will make a difference in your Christian life and will change the eternal experience for many with whom you will share. Bill Fay reminds us, "God can use your words, He can't use your silence." God help us to be active in sharing our faith—Philemon 6.

> —**Bruce Schoeman**, Encore Ministries

... Just like Jesus, Tom's passion is souls and He has been given creative ways to reach the lost in non-offensive ways that many can easily grab ahold of and put into practice... You will be blessed by reading and putting into practice what Tom shares in *SCARY FUN!*

> —**Mark R. Anderson**, Evangelist, Missionary & Author of
> *Humility the Hidden Key to Walking in Signs and Wonders*

Introduction—Ignite The Fire

IGNITE THE FIRE

My great-grandpa was the town drunk. Someone shared the love of Jesus with this wife-beating alcoholic. As a result, I am writing this book you are about to read. I hope to meet that someone in heaven someday and thank him/her for speaking up. But until then, I have decided to also speak up, hoping I can help rescue many more!

Overall, I think I do a good job at a number of things. But some things I don't do very well at. As hard as I try, sometimes things just don't work out. I'm hoping you will think different of this, my first book… *"Scary Fun!"*

For example, my kids tell me I am a horrible cook. I'm not so sure they're right, but I have noticed whenever I cook, our dog goes to the neighbor's house to eat.

In my early years of marriage, I would tease my slender wife by putting my arm around her waist and squeezing any little amount of extra around her waist. She hated it. One day while shopping, I was standing next to her as she looked at some clothes. In all of five seconds while I looked away, she walked away, and a different woman moved into her exact place. While still looking away, I put my arm around her waist. But something felt wrong. There was a lot more to squeeze than usual! I looked down to see a different woman staring at me in horror. I quickly yelled for my wife and was promptly cured of my teasing habit.

Years later while waiting to tee off our first round of golf for the season, the gallery was packed with golfers. Each was waiting their turn. In front of us were four women. I laughed to myself thinking, *"these ladies can't hit very well."* My turn finally came, and to my utter horror my tee shot took a 90 degree right angle into the parking lot. Clunk, clunk, clunk was the sound as it careened off several cars. But I would not be deterred. The crowd was perfectly quiet, but I knew they were now all laughing at me. So I mustered all the remaining courage I had, and shot a second ball. But again I couldn't see where it went. Clunk, clunk, clunk told me it had again hit someone's car. This time I simply took a third golf ball and threw it out onto the fairway. The game of golf had once again humbled me to my core.

So, what makes me think I will do any better writing this book?

Because my dog came home, my wife is still with me, and I gave up golf.

And because the thoughts I will share with you are not dead and lifeless theory. They have been birthed in me, and are daily proof I am living the greatest adventure of my life right now!

I am honored you would let me speak these thoughts into your life. So here we go…

⸻

- ➢ If you knew of a way to double your fruitfulness in Christ, would you be interested?

- ➢ If I could tell you of something that could greatly increase your fulfillment as a Christian, would you be interested?

- ➢ If I told you over ½ million people worldwide have already said this was a turning point in their walk with Christ, would you be interested in learning more?

- ➢ If your success in this was not determined by age, education, money or intelligence, would you be interested?

If you're like most people, you would shout "YES, please tell me!"

Have you looked deeply at the people of your world recently? Most are stressed out. And everyone is looking for inner peace and purpose, the very things you and I possess! Yet many Christians are just as depressed, lonely and frustrated with life as the non-Christians appear.

I am excited to tell you I crossed a threshold some time ago that is reflected in this book. I decided I was not satisfied with just singing and preaching about changing my world. I wanted to do something about it. I wanted my fire for the Lord burning brightly. And I knew if I focused on giving to others, the blessing would also return to me. So I made a crucial, life-altering decision.

I decided to speak up. I decided to change my world one day at a time. I decided to take this good news outside my church and into my marketplace... everyday I could.

For this reason, I'd like to tell you about a phone call I had with a computer repairman in the USA. As we were waiting for a download on my computer, I decided again to speak up, using the tool I will introduce to you later on in the book. I asked him, "What is the best thing that has ever happened to you in your lifetime?"

He seemed cautiously eager to answer my question, but first said, "Do you really want to know"? I said "yes"! He then said something that completely shocked me. He said, "the best thing in my life happened when I received a surgical sex-change operation."

I was stunned... a *sex-change operation*? I almost dropped the phone. My computer repairman was sharing real personal info with me. I had never met the guy, and now he's telling me this?

Everything within me cried "TMI, TMI" (Too Much Information!). I immediately breathed a prayer and asked God for wisdom. I didn't want to mess up this divine opportunity. He talked about it a little more, and I reluctantly listened, as I was still in shock.

But then he said, "and what's the best thing in your life?" And I said, "Do you really want to know?" And he said "yes".

So I began to tell him how I was once looking for purpose and real love, but that I had found it in Jesus Christ. I told him how my life was now filled with joy, purpose and the promise of heaven. He became very silent, but was listening intently.

Then we finished our computer business. But at the end of the call, he said something I will never forget. His last parting words to me on the phone were unforgettable…

… "Will you pray for me?"

My friend, there is no greater joy for a Jesus-lover than to help someone else in their search for God's love. It will exhilarate you beyond belief. It will bring new purpose to your earthly life. Your days will not be boring anymore. You will enter God's best for you. It will ignite your spiritual fire!

That's why I wrote this book. Leviticus 6:13 (NIV) says,

"The fire must be kept burning on the altar continuously, it must not go out."

The Old Testament priests were always to keep the fire stoked, ready to receive another animal sacrifice for the people's sins. The analogy is clear. We believers in Jesus Christ are now priests unto God according to Revelation 1:6. We are to always keep the fire and

passion for His presence burning brightly inside of us.
So whether your fire is waning or burning brightly, reading this
book can help you to go to the next level. Someday we will stand
before God and give account of what we did with this wonderful
relationship with Jesus while on earth. I pray we will not only enjoy
Heaven, but we will have much fruit to lay before the Lord because
our spiritual fire was ignited and burning brightly, influencing many
with His great love!

Is this scary? Absolutely. But is it both scary *and* fun? Read on if
you want to know the answer. If you love Jesus, you are about to
experience life's greatest adventure! It's time to ignite the fire!

Tom Elie

1

JOIN THE CLUB

Quote to remember: *"... I think the biggest problem in the church is this awkwardness. We just don't know how to converse with people. We're scared to do it, so we don't do it." ~Francis Chan*

I had just returned to the USA from another exciting trip to India when we had a fierce thunderstorm. It was so strong it knocked out my computer. I called my computer company, and they linked me to a customer service center in the Philippine Islands. (I am told they teach their workers western accents so westerners feel more cared for.) While waiting for my computer to update, I felt this nudge from the Holy Spirit to share my faith with the woman who was helping me. She was very helpful, very bubbly in her personality and very talkative. So I asked her what was the best thing that had ever happened to her in her lifetime. She eagerly said her family was the best thing in her life. After she finished I asked, "May I share the best thing that ever happened to me?" She quickly said, "Yes!"

I responded by saying I too was very blessed… with a great wife and four sons, but that was not the greatest thing. I told her there was a time in my life when I had no peace, and I was looking for my purpose on earth. Then I told how Christ changed my life and gave me the purpose and meaning for which I was searching. But something was wrong. While I was talking, I noticed she went completely silent. The bubbly personality had vanished. The call ended very cordially, and at the end of the call she humbly added, "and thank you, sir, for the nice words."

Two days later I received an email from her. I had not given her my email address, so she had to look it up in their company records. Here's her surprising note to me:

> *"Dear Mr. Elie,*
> *It is highly prohibited for us to contact our customers.*
> *However when you were telling me how Christ changed*
> *your life, my eyes were showering with tears. I could*
> *not even talk because my voice would crack. When I*
> *was 17 years old I was serving God. But just yesterday,*
> *I told God He might be for some people, but He is not*
> *for me. Then today you called. I am overwhelmed to*
> *think that one day later, out of all the thousands of calls*
> *we receive, God directed your call to me. Thank you for*
> *sharing how Jesus changed your life. Thank you, thank*
> *you, thank you."*

Wow! I was so excited! Thank God I didn't get so consumed with my computer problem that I missed a golden opportunity. My simple willingness to speak up was used by God to help a young woman in a spiritual crisis of her own. God loves to use earthly humans to be His heavenly ambassadors. Had I not I received her email, I never would have known how timely my obedience was.

But one day the sowers and the reapers will see all the fruits of their combined witness, and rejoice together in heaven!
Listen to John 4:36:

> "And he who reaps receives wages, and gathers fruit
> for eternal life, that both he who sows and he who reaps
> may rejoice together."

Today, masses of people are looking for hope. And we have what they desire. It is such a tremendous joy to purposely engage people in eternal conversations.

Several years ago God confronted me. I felt Him asking me why I was not regularly sharing my faith outside of my clergy role? I was seeing many come to Christ in our India and Africa Gospel and Healing Festivals. I was preaching in American pulpits. But seldom did I go out of my way to engage unbelievers in conversation, like Jesus did with the woman at the well in John chapter four. Seldom did I follow the example of Paul who shared daily in the marketplace with those who happened to be there. (Acts 17:17 "Therefore he reasoned in the synagogue with the Jews and with the Gentile worshipers, and in the marketplace daily with those who happened to be there.")

By God's grace we had seen much fruit in our ministry. But the Lord says when a vine is fruitful, He prunes it so it can produce even more fruit. The pruning is never fun, but the results can be amazing. Little did I know my Christian life and fruitfulness were about to radically change for the better.

God and I started having a serious discussion. I started giving God my lame excuses as to why I could not or should not be more public in sharing my faith. But He gently reminded me of the alcoholism in my ancestors, and how it easily could have been my destiny too. Finally I gave up and gave in to His compassion. So I made a bargain with God. I told Him if He gave me a faith-sharing tool that worked, treated people with respect, and was fruitful, I would do it. And He agreed.

So then I did something totally scary. I took a challenge to share my faith everyday for *seven* days in a row. Why did this scare me so? I have preached in front of many thousands of people. I have led many to the Lord face-to-face. I have gone door-to-door more times than I care to remember. Why would this challenge me so?

> ➢ Perhaps because I knew defeating my fears could change my life forever.

> ➢ Perhaps because I was dissatisfied with limiting my influence to the pulpit.

> ➢ Perhaps because compassion for the unreached was filling my heart.

> ➢ Perhaps because my capacity for risk for Christ was not satisfied.

And so I began my "scary week." My friend, Pastor George Bunnell, said he would do it with me. George was always ready to tell someone about the God he loved. And we were both excited!

On day one, I was driving home on Monday night after a full day at the Oasis World Ministries offices. I had not even thought of my seven-day challenge. I had been with my Christian office, Christian computer, Christian emails, Christian staff, and Christian telephone. Now I was going home for the evening to be with my Christian wife, Christian family, Christian TV and Christian magazines. Suddenly my memory-lapse stopped. In horror, I realized I had forgotten about my heart-felt pledge to share my faith everyday for seven days. I knew I certainly could not allow myself to fail on the first day. So I pulled my car into a gasoline station even though I needed no gas. I went inside to see whom I could talk to. I just had to be around some non-Christians!

I got in line to buy a newspaper, hoping I could at least be the last in line so I could talk with the clerk at the counter. But while I was standing in line, I looked to my right. There stood a man by the cookies just staring into space. He was not shopping. Just staring. I noticed a necklace with a cross hanging around his neck. And then the light bulb turned on in my head. His cross necklace was my perfect invitation to share my faith!

So I approached him and complimented him on his cross necklace. I asked him what it meant to him. He said his grandmother had given it to him. That told me two things. First, I knew he probably had a praying grandma! And secondly, I knew I was about to be an answer to his grandma's prayers!

I asked him if I could share what his cross meant to me? He agreed. And for the next 10 minutes he eagerly listened as I shared how Christ changed my life. I was amazed. I didn't think Americans were this open to hearing the gospel. And I was so excited I didn't fail my first day. But I thought it was both scary and fun at the same time!

And after seven days, I was still amazed. This faith-sharing idea really worked! I did not talk to seven people, but I talked to eleven people in one week! The delivery truck driver, a store manager and employee, a customer while shopping, and many others. I had never done this outside of my clergy role. I was thrilled.

My partner, Pastor George, and I both decided this was too good to stop, so we committed to do another seven days. And after that we said, 'let's finish out the month'. And after that we said something I never thought we could say...

"Let's never stop sharing. Let's try to share our faith everyday for the rest of our lives!"

At that moment in October of 2003, history was made in our hearts.

And years later I still have a goal of sharing my faith everyday. Pastor George and I still encourage each other in prayer and text each other when we have had a great opportunity to share our faith. Just last night, I had the privilege of praying with Alicia, my waitress, to receive the Lord as her Savior. She was so excited... and so was I.

The principles listed in this book have revolutionized my faith in Christ. And I am still growing every day I use it. It has restored great joy to my faith, and protects me from the terrible conditions of being nominal, lukewarm, or even backsliding. The adventure is awesome. And by God's grace, I will never stop.

But, there's an elephant in the room.

According to Wikipedia, "'Elephant in the room' is an English metaphorical idiom for an obvious truth that is either being ignored or going unaddressed. The idiomatic expression also applies to an obvious problem or risk no one wants to discuss.

It is based on the idea that an elephant in a room would be impossible to overlook; thus, people in the room who pretend the elephant is not there have chosen to avoid dealing with the looming big issue."

And here it is...

A recent survey by a leading evangelical denomination found a startling statistic. According to current trends, 97% of the Christians they surveyed will never share the plan of salvation with one unbeliever... ever. That's right, not even once in their entire lifetime.

Another source noted that only 4% of pastors feel equipped to share their faith, and only 6% of Christians feel equipped. That, coupled with the our educated guess that around 90% of unbelievers will never attend our churches, means the future of the church is in big trouble.

Do you find this hard to believe? Let me prove it to you right now. Answer this revealing question:

> "How many people have tried to witness to you personally about their faith in Jesus Christ, thinking you were an unbeliever?"

Be honest now. Many people say "0-3". Most say "0". We may talk about God occasionally or even invite someone to attend our church. But most don't feel equipped to share the plan of salvation with even one friend.

And here's another quote from Thom Ranier, president of LifeWay Christian Resources:

> "Nine out of ten churches in America are either declining or growing more slowly than the communities in which they are located. In other words, most churches are losing ground in their communities."

THIS MUST CHANGE.

One thing is certain… both Christians and non-Christians are uncomfortable with evangelism.

But the Mormons are intentional about sharing their faith… every male is required to be a missionary for two years. And the Jehovah Witnesses share their faith regularly… out of duty.

But God took a big risk. He demonstrated His love to us, hoping we would do the same for others He loves. In fact, He said as much:

"love one another as I have loved you." (John 15:12)
So do our systems need some updating? Are we losing our first love? WE MUST TALK ABOUT IT. I must begin by asking difficult questions of myself and others that hopefully will help us identify the problem, so we can begin our journey.

- ➤ Should we keep pretending we are really reaching our sphere of influence?

- ➤ Should we support missionaries without also sharing our faith ourselves?

- ➤ Should we be satisfied with reaching a small percentage of our city with the gospel?

  OR…

  Should we gracefully talk about the elephant in the room?

As evangelist Bill Fay said, "Remember, God can use your words, but He cannot use your silence."

So here's 4 life-changing questions. Once identified and talked about, the answers can help us discover life's greatest adventure!

1. Are you like many who are dissatisfied with 'nominal, Sunday-only Christianity'?

2. Do you feel you have the "guilt" of evangelism rather than the "joy" of evangelism?

3. Do you wish the fire you once had for Jesus could burn bright again?

4. Do you wonder what God's real purpose is for you on earth?

If so, please know you aren't alone.

Join the club of Christians who know there must be more. But let me be clear. This book is not written to belittle any church or person. The problem is simply that we have forgotten what it's like to really be in love. We look to other people as if it is their job to make us happy. Our entitlement culture says we deserve better... a better spouse, a better pastor, a better job, a better community, a better country, a better president, a better church, etc. But Jesus promised us an abundant life if we do it His way... working together with Him.

The principles listed in this book have the potential to radically and exponentially change your life, and the lives of countless others, forever. In fact, a *new you* can evolve. Your life can be full of peace and joy, while giving the same to others everyday.

Does this sound too good to be true?

I'm not a multi-level marketer. I'm not trying to hype you or play on your emotions. What's described cannot be bought. You won't find it on eBay. It's not a scam. It's not seasonal or just for a select few, gifted or lucky folk. What I am describing has worked for myself and many others. And it works whenever I put it into action.

It is not a respecter of how much you are worth, how much education you have, your knowledge of the Bible or your family history. It doesn't care how bad or good of a person you have been. It doesn't take into consideration how many times you have failed in life or in relationships.

It works for all races of humanity in every country on earth. It is cross-cultural to the max. It works for every age group, both genders, and is usable wherever you are right now.
There are no limits… except ourselves!

This doesn't depend on your personality or your charisma. It isn't a "system" that only works for a few people. It won't leave you disappointed once you apply its principles.

However, it will take work, and at times will be scary. You will be stretched further than you thought imaginable. But it will also bring more joy than you ever thought possible! And it will bring a new sense of adventure everyday if you desire it. In fact, your life will never seem boring again. I guarantee it.

If what I've described seems appealing to you, then you are a candidate for change. You don't even have to change yourself. You just need to ask God to change you with His power.

You see, God has promised to do super-natural things in our lives. Listen to the awesome verse:

"Now unto him that is able to do exceeding abundantly
above all that we ask or think, according to the power
that worketh in us, to Him *be* glory..." Ephesians 3:20-21

I am not a Greek scholar, but let me unfold this verse to you in a
fresh way. The word "exceedingly" in Greek "huper," which means
"more than." The word "abundantly" in Greek is *"perissos,"*
meaning *"beyond."* Are you getting the picture? God says He is
able to do "more than" we ask or think, and even "beyond more
than" we ask or think. And how is it done? Simply by the power of
the Holy Spirit that resides in us. So go ahead, take your best shot
at what you think God could do through you, and you are not even
close!

Ready to get off the spiritual treadmill and see God use you? You
don't have to go on a missions trip to see this happen. Life becomes
one big exciting missions trip!

These principles, if applied, will help you enjoy your faith in Jesus
like never before. In fact, you will return to your first love. You will
be like a kid in a dollar store with ten dollars to spend!

So, what are we talking about?

Promise me you won't shut the book immediately when I tell you
what this book is all about. If you do, you may never experience
what I am really describing. If you say, "I know all about that," and
write it off as another tool that only works for a few people, you
will miss one of the greatest opportunities to see real and satisfying
growth in your life.

After the 2010 catastrophic earthquake in Haiti, a young woman
told her amazing story. She said that coming to Haiti to help the

hopeless was the best thing that had ever happened to her. She personally paid for $9,000 worth of relief and medical supplies to help the helpless. She publicly confessed her expensive "shoe-fettish," and said she is done being so selfish. She was going to change her lifestyle because she had found the secret of giving to others.

Likewise, this book will help you fulfill your God-given desire to give others the greatest gift possible... His great love. Yes, this book will motivate and equip you to share the love of God that is in you with people all around you who are *desperate* for a second chance in life... a fresh start.

The psalmist David said, "Restore to me the joy of Your salvation, And uphold me *by Your* generous spirit. *Then* I will teach transgressors Your ways, And sinners shall be converted to You." (Psalm 51:12-13).
This passage is in the middle of David's prayer of repentance for adultery. He had lost his way. His focus had become self-centered, instead of God-centered. He was building his own kingdom rather than God's. But now he is returning to his first love... a fresh start. That's what we need... a fresh start!

I want to help you start fresh by giving you a tool you can use right away to make a difference. It will give you websites that will instruct you, and websites that you can point others to. It introduces a video that will equip you in a simple, but profound tool that has been proven time and again to relate to people right where they are.

This tool is not rude or pushy. It treats people the way you would want to be treated. Yet it is intentional and loving at the same time. People will be intrigued with the question when you ask them to recall the greatest thing that has ever happened to them. They will smile as they access their memory archives for some good experiences. Then they will sincerely listen as you speak from your heart about the wonderful hope God has birthed in you.

Ready for change? Why waste another day of this great gift called life? Get your pen out and underline the things God speaks to you. It can change your life, and countless others!

I challenge you to experience life's greatest adventure. I promise it will be both scary... and fun!

Question to ponder:
What are the main factors that keep you from sharing your faith the way you would like?

_____

_____

_____

_____

_____

Action Steps:
Write down what has helped you take steps of faith outside your own comfort zone.

_____

_____

_____

_____

_____

2

IT'S ALL *THEIR* FAULT!

Quote to remember: *"What gives anyone the right to hear the gospel twice before everyone has heard it once?"* Oswald J. Smith

(Author's note: Can you allow me one chapter to paint a verbal picture of the problem I see? Sometimes we have to identify the problem clearly before we can hear the summons to find a solution. And there is a very positive solution! Thanks.)

It's all *their* fault. I've seen way too much. I can't go back now. It's too late. They've spoiled me.

Why can't I just live a normal, average Christian life? Then I wouldn't have these haunting thoughts. But I can't… and it's all because of *them*.

Perhaps it started in Montego Bay, Jamaica. I was only 16 years old. In one short month our team of humble teenagers fearfully walked from hut-to-hut and prayed with 500 spiritually-hungry people to receive Jesus as their Savior! Culture shock and all, we came home spiritually invigorated.

Maybe it was Mexico City where I held my first open-air gospel street meeting. In one night we saw many freely accept Christ, along with 70 people openly testifying of being healed from their sicknesses. I didn't believe them, so I again asked who was healed. The same hands went up. I realized right then that Jesus wants to use healing as an evangelistic tool. I had never seen anything like this in America.

Or maybe it was the neighborhood slums of Gitturai 44 outside of Nairobi, Kenya. Thousands of Africans stood for hours in the open-air field to eagerly hear the gospel of Jesus. That's right, *stood*, not sat. And many turned their lives to Christ.

It's surely also been India. In many places like the Dharavi slums (where the movie *Slumdog Millionaire* was based), we've seen hundreds of thousands of Hindus confess their sin and turn to the One True God, Jesus Christ. People bring their own anointing oil for their sicknesses. Blind eyes open... the deaf hear... the lame walk. Twice at our altars, 250 people stood in the pouring rain to receive Jesus as their Lord, and I stood in amazement.

They're desperate. They're humble. And I am not. That's my problem. I'm ruined to settle for anything less. I've seen too much now. There's no going back. So it's all *their* fault.

I watch New Testament Christianity being lived out in these developing nations. It's refreshing, invigorating and energizing! They use the faith they have. The church sings with their whole heart. They endure persecution. They laugh at simple jokes.

They're relational. They honor their elders. Children play with sticks in the dirt, and they're happy. It's a simple, but hard life. Yet their smiles are downright contagious. They earn two to three dollars per day, yet they rejoice in the Lord. The church is growing by leaps and bounds.

And I am jealous. (God forgive me.)

But each time my plane lands in the America that I dearly love, I see myself differently. Each time I return from the third-world nations of the world, I know one thing... I must change. My heart must soften, or it will harden forever. I see the thin layer of cynicism that surrounds my culture. I see the glitzy, alluring and provocative ads that promise what they can never deliver. I feel the strained relationships. I hear the whine of the entitlement mentality of my prideful and selfish generation. I feel the apathy of our church culture, and again I hear the church gossip. And with the force of a strong magnetic field, I feel myself sucked back into normal western-Christianity. The America I love is in deep trouble. And so am I.

I think we can all see it to some degree. Watching the news is downright depressing. Our moral decline has shifted into high gear. We are on slippery slopes headed for a certain and major wipeout. Our families are broken. Our schools need metal-detectors for security reasons. We're dumbing down in so many ways. Pornography websites are the most often visited sites on the internet. Our nation is in runaway debt, and we consumers are following the lead. We have under-estimated the influence of our western media upon ourselves, and the whole world. We love entertainment, and hate personal discipline.

So, what's the solution?

Give me someone to blame, and I will at least feel better. Blame the Democrats. Ridicule the Republicans. Get a new president, a different congress, a different spouse, or a different job. Throw more money at our problems. Give someone else a bailout. Build more prisons. Find a new church.

But we've tried all that. And we're getting worse.

And what about the American church? Think of it. Most of the church growth in the world today is happening in emerging nations like India, China, Indonesia and the Philippines. The only places where the church is NOT growing are North America and Europe.

When you read the next paragraph, please don't think I am trying to be critical or holier-than-thou. I'm not trying to lay a 'guilt-trip' on you. After more than sixty international ministry trips, I just see my country of America differently than I used to. I am so very thankful for my country, my freedoms and my abundant blessings. I am grateful for the religious heritage I have enjoyed. I am thankful that America is still the most giving nation on the earth. What I say, I say because I want my country back. I don't want to live in the past, but I believe its future is in very critical condition. I believe the best is yet to come... but only if we change... and quickly.

America has only 5% of the world's population, yet has enjoyed up to 50% of the world's wealth. We have most of the world's clergy and churches. Yet I am told there is very little, if any, positive net church growth in the last 10 years. One major protestant denomination's own internal study shows that one-half of their adherents have not come to a personal born-again relationship with Jesus as their Lord and Savior. The heart-passion for Jesus has left many churches, and nominal Christianity has hardened hearts like concrete. Think of it... a hard-core, Bible-believing movement that has missed one-half of their own pew-sitting people. Another major protestant Pentecostal movement received 60 million dollars in giving in one US state last year, yet the church movement declined in numbers. Think of it... 60 million dollars given to God, and no net church growth. One transparent national, evangelical denominational president recently wrote,

> *"Unfortunately the greater majority of our churches are not growing. Why? Could it be because we, as leaders, are tasked more with comforting the saints than challenging and discipling them to reach the lost? (George Wood, January 2013 Minister's Newsletter)*

You see, the real answers to America's root problems are not found in the White House. They're supposed to be found in the church house. But if much of the church is sleeping, what hope does a country then have? The Bible says in Hebrews 9:27 that all people will one day be judged by God. But He also said in 1 Peter 4:17 that judgment begins at the house of God. That concerns me. And I would guess it concerns you too.

For too long I have waffled between what one author calls being a "worldly Christian" and a "world-class Christian." *Worldly Christians* continually ask God what He can do for them. *World-class Christians* ask God what they can do for Him. The former is in it for what they can get out of it, and the latter is in it because God has already done enough for them at Calvary.

I thought, "What can I do? I'm just one person. I can't change the world." And I was right.

From all my years in pastoral ministry, I've learned one very important lesson: I cannot make people change. I can, and should, influence others. But I can only change me. Period.

So, I take the blame. It's really my 'fault. And I apologize.

At times I am weak, timid, insecure, scared and intimidated. And God says, "Good! I like to use weak people to put to shame the mighty. I like to use the foolish things of the world to confound the wise. I like to use nobodies. (See 1 Corinthians 1:27. I paraphrased.) And in 2 Corinthians 12:9 Paul writes, "My strength is made perfect in your weakness." When we are a nobody, and God is the Somebody, we don't steal the credit due Him. And God loves that. If we start taking the credit, God knows our pride will again be our undoing. And we will end up, well, like we are today. Personally, I see only three possible solutions for the spiritual and moral healing of a nation:

1. **A major and sustained economic collapse.** Greed is certainly one of our gods, and it must fall. When it does, that nation will fall to its knees again in humility.

2. **The loss of our religious freedoms.** The persecuted church always thrives.

3. **Sharing authentic faith outside the church building.** Christianity is highly contagious, but only if it comes outside the church.

Neither you nor I want the first two options. But the third option requires change.

Before you put this book down and decide this is for someone else, please read the next paragraph.

Like I said earlier, a recent Protestant survey of a major USA denomination found an alarming statistic. According to current trends, 97% of their Christian born-again people will never share the plan of salvation with an unbeliever... ever. Not in their entire lifetime.

Can you imagine what would happen if 97% of parents never bore children? Our civilization would die. And that is exactly is what is happening to the church.

So, what is our hope?

- We will surely change if we experience economic collapse. We will fall to our knees once again.
- We will be forced to change if we lose our religious freedoms, and the church goes underground.
  The persecuted church always grows... eventually.
- Or, we must willingly change now, and decide we have a faith worth sharing.

We must take the compassion of Jesus into our neighborhoods and into the marketplace... into our community leaders, our families, our loved ones, our school mates, our co-workers and our friends. We must repent of our spiritual apathy. We must repent for our sins. We must change intentionally, or we may be forced to change. As my friend Bruce Schoeman says, "Take change by the hand before it takes you by the throat."

So, this book is about *change*.

About now you may be starting to feel guilty. That's not the purpose of this book. But the devil has lied to the church. He says, "You don't have the gift of evangelism." Most Christians I know have the *guilt* of evangelism. They feel real guilty when they read stuff like this. But nowhere in the Bible is the *gift of evangelism* even mentioned. In fact, the office of the evangelist is mentioned in Ephesians 4:11, but their job is to equip the saints for the work of the ministry. Only the *commission*... the *mandate is mentioned for us all*. In Mark 16:15, He told us all to "go" into all the world and make a difference. Scary? Yes. But when we go, He goes with us. We are never alone.

God used all kinds of weak and foolish people to advance His message. Moses stuttered. Abraham doubted God's promise. David committed adultery and murder. Samson compromised. Gideon was the least in his clan. Peter denied the Lord... three times. The disciples were common fishermen. These weren't all *type A* personalities. They were shy, timid, insecure and impetuous at times... just like you and I.

Today, the happiest people I see are those who are making an eternal difference for Christ with their lives. When I personally share my faith, my fire for the Lord is ignited, and I am energized. I return to my first love!

But we have a problem. Recently I was in a Florida restaurant enjoying food with some good friends. Our waitress, named Natasha, was articulate, well-trained and seemed to be poised and humbly confident. After sharing our faith with her, she admitted she too was a strong believer in Jesus, but was afraid to admit it to us. I inquired, "how long have you been a waitress?" She replied, "For 12 years." I asked, "Have any of your customers ever shared their faith verbally with you before?" She said, "A few have left some tracts, but today is the first time in 12 years that anyone has told me about Jesus."

I turned in my rental car at Alamo and struck up a conversation with the attendant. He turned out to be a committed Christian. He also said that after five months of working there, no one had ever shared their faith with him.

I saw a homeless lady holding a sign at an intersection. The sign said, *"Homeless and Hungry."* After driving ½ mile past her, I decided I would make a difference. I bought a sandwich and an apple, and drove back to where she was standing. As I pulled into a business near her, I saw several other homeless men sitting on the curb eating some sandwiches. I thought, *"Oh great, another scam. She stands out there and pulls on our heart-strings, and these men get her food."* But no! She said the food was for her, and that she had been homeless for 5 months. She also turned out to be a Christian who had never been witnessed to in all her time standing on the street corners. I was so glad I didn't listen to my judgmental bent. God knows I have missed many more opportunities than I have taken. I was so glad I simply cared enough to help.

We tend to think someone else has surely reached out to them. Or, like me, we can think our own efforts to be kind will be in vain. But a recent Barna Research survey showed that 75% of Americans want to be close to God. What an invitation!

And my personal Bible "survey" reveals that 100% of the angels rejoice when even one sinner repents of his sin! How awesome is that?

Jesus is all about improving our lives. He wants to change us for the positive. Are you tired of a status quo, boring religion? Don't you want to see God change our country? Will you be cleverly sucked into our culture, or will you transform the culture you live in? We decide daily if we will repent of living for our selfish agenda. We decide daily if we will embrace the cross and live for the salvation of others. This is where you and I find fulfillment!

Of course, right about now our old flesh and/or the devil will try to shame us or condemn us. He will tell us we are a miserable failure as a Christian. He will try to get us to compare ourselves with others, which Paul says is not wise (2 Corinthians 10:12). No one is trying to condemn you except the devil himself. Remember, condemnation is destructive, and conviction is constructive. The devil condemns, and the Holy Spirit convicts!

So how will you, the holder of good news, respond to a desperate world? Decisions… decisions.

The choice is ours. Our world depends on us... the light-bearers, the salt of the earth, the ambassadors of heaven. We, the church of Jesus, hold the key to our country's future and our own. We are the watchmen on the wall. It's time to sound the trumpet. It's time to come outside of the church. The ship is sinking fast. Hurry, we need you! Will you take part in life's greatest adventure?

Questions to ponder:

Will you make the choice today to go to the next level?

Will you ask the Holy Spirit to do His complete work in you, starting now?

Will you join the adventure and embrace personal change?

Action step:

Pray, and then write down a name that you could ask to read this book and take this journey with you. Two are better than one!

3

DO IT AFRAID!

Quote to remember: *"When we step out of our comfort zone, we are stepping into God's comfort zone."* ~Bruce Schoeman

I used to be addicted. Not to meth or crack or cocaine. Not alcohol either. Believe it or not, riding a scary roller coaster can be addicting. As a kid I loved the thrill, the adrenaline rush, the scariness and the simple fact that I was facing my fears. The bigger, the better. Alright, maybe I wasn't officially addicted, but it sure beat doing homework! However, around 30 years old, an internal switch was turned off. Now instead of loving the rush, I actually loathe it. It was like night and day. Go figure.

Roller-coaster junkies abound. They travel around the country looking to ride the biggest and the best, as if they were climbing Mount Everest.

Here's the process of what happens. They eagerly arrive at the amusement park, stare at how high the tracks are above their heads and hear the screams of the current riders in their cars. They desire to do something daring, and their friends encourage them. After a good three or four seconds of serious thought, they somehow convince themselves that they can do it. They get securely strapped into their car, and realize there is now no turning back. They hear the clickety-clack of the track as their car slowly plods up the first hill. And then they face their worst fears. The drop-off looks bigger than they imagined. But like it or not, they're going down... they are well beyond the point of no return. As they begin their descent, they feel the heart-stopping panic that accompanies every rider when their car picks up speed. The wind is rushing through their hair, and they are white-knuckling it all the way down. They hear their voice join the chorus of others in a blood-curdling scream that really means, "What have I gotten myself into?!"

When it's all over, and the ride has stopped, they exit, feeling nauseous, exhausted and like they cheated death. But in their eyes they have now entered the class of super-heroes! They conquered their fears.

Then the most remarkable thought enters their mind:

"That was a blast... let's do it again!"

And they do it. Again, and again, and again. And pretty soon they are bored with what originally brought them great fear. They begin to look for even bigger roller coasters to conquer. And on it goes.

One pastor told me that sharing your faith is a lot like the roller-coaster syndrome. You're scared to death before you do it. You commit yourself to the point of no-return; you stumble over your words for the first few times, and when you're all done you say, "Wow, I did it. That was exhilarating... Let's do it again!"

We do an evangelistic outreach called *Gas Buydown* at local gas stations. Everywhere we go and every group who has participated have felt all of the above. Fear, intimidation, panic, insecurity and shyness have been our common phobias. Yet, after two hours of training and two hours of outreach, they feel stimulated, empowered, confident and secure. Pardon the pun, but they feel pumped! And believe it or not, they want to do it again!

If you think I'm hyping this, or don't quite believe me, check out people's responses at our website www.gasbuydown.org.

The thrill of overcoming our fears is empowering and exhilarating. Once you've been there, you wonder what held you back so long. You're never quite the same again.

So, may I ask you some questions?

1. Are you really satisfied with a predictable faith that's usually about "me," OR do you want to go out in a flash, burning hot for God until the finish line?

2. Did you sign up for boring Christianity, OR did you sign up to really enjoy this new life in Christ?

Billy Graham has been quoted as saying he got nervous butterflies in his stomach every time he stepped into the pulpit to preach. In other words, it's OK to be afraid. I think FEAR is really "False Evidence Appearing Real." When you realize your fears often try to keep you from your divine potential, they are much less intimidating.

Teacher Joyce Meyers tells us to "Do it afraid!" In other words, "Get back on the roler coaster!" Stop letting your fears rule you. Enjoy living on the edge!

Someone once said that "faith" is spelled R-I-S-K. Someone else said the Chinese meaning for "risk" is *dangerous opportunity*. Let's face it, walking is really controlled-falling. Everyday we habitually are involved in things that once seemed quite risky to us. Our first solo bicycle ride, driving the car for the first time, our first kiss, our first broken relationship, our first job interview, our first airplane ride, our first cross-cultural missions trip, our first time tithing, our first child, our new business start-up, our first teenager, and so on. There are so many *firsts* in our lives. It's only when you become grandparents that you can actually start relaxing!

I will never forget my first sermon. I was the minister of music at one of the first mega-churches in Minneapolis, Minnesota, USA. I was accustomed to singing and testifying in front of thousands of people every week. There was no fear in me, only an excitement of what God was going to do in each church service.

But delivering my first sermon was quite different. It was a Wednesday night with about 200 adults gathered together. I was very excited and a little nervous. But I had no idea what I was about to face. After the usual praise and worship time, they had the announcements and offering. And then someone introduced me as the speaker. I am sure the people were surprised, because they did not know me in this role. I felt I was well-prepared, and I confidently stepped into the pulpit.
I looked up with eagerness in my heart to deliver my first sermon. But when I looked into the congregation's eyes, I suddenly felt my own inadequacy. I thought, "These people are looking to me for a word from the Lord. I am sure I will not be as good as the senior

pastors who usually speak. I wonder if they will get anything out of my message." A wave of panic hit me like a ton of bricks.

I was not accustomed to such a feeling of total helplessness and paralysis. I didn't know what to do. I could only think of two possibilities-either turn to my right and run as fast as I could off this stage and never, ever return to a pulpit again... or run squarely toward my fears. I'm sure it was only a few seconds that I was pondering this, but it seemed a lot longer.

At the moment, the first option looked better. But the fact that my sermon topic was *"The Fear of Failure"* seemed to help catapult me past my fears. I decided to go for broke. I thought I had nothing to lose, so I ran directly toward my fear.

And do you know what happened? Within a few seconds my fear started subsiding, and within 60 seconds my fear was completely gone. It was absolutely amazing to me that I could go from one extreme to the other solely based on my feelings. I learned much later that "feelings are not always my friend." If I would have listened to my feelings, perhaps I never would have preached again. It would have certainly been an even bigger mountain to climb the next time.

But I didn't yield to my feelings. Instead I listened to the Holy Spirit. "For God has not given us a spirit of fear, but of power and of love and of a sound mind" (2 Timothy 1:7). As soon as I made up my mind not to run, I felt empowered. It was like God pouring renewed confidence within me like you would fill a pitcher of water. It was definitely a work of the Holy Spirit, and I knew it.

You see, I had forgotten the fears I once faced when I sang my first song, or played piano publicly for the first time. I was now a pro at it and felt very comfortable. But I had forgotten that skills are developed and not just gifted.

When I was done preaching, I felt a sense of relief. I thought, "It's a good thing I don't get paid to preach. I will go back to my music ministry now." But there was a seasoned missionary and Bible teacher, Earl Quesnell, on the platform listening to my sermon. When I was done I walked off the stage, glad to be finished. But pastor Earl wanted to speak to me. I will never forget the seemingly ludicrous thing he said to me.

> "Tom, you did a good job for your first sermon. But there will come a time when you will be known more for your preaching than you are for your music."

I shyly thanked him and thought to myself, "Boy did you miss that one Earl. I know God uses you prophetically, but I think you are way off on this one." Little did I know that one day I would be preaching to much larger crowds around the world than I ever sang to before. Pastor Earl saw beyond my fear. He heard from God.

This was unimaginable to me. But eventually the prophetic word of the Lord came to pass! What if I had given in to my fear? For the Lord's will to happen, we have to intentionally follow Him and take steps of faith that will help launch His plan into action.

So, to which voice are you listening, fear or faith? The voice of fear is strong and intimidating. But the voice of God is stronger and invigorating. Both involve R-I-S-K. Fear risks never knowing or becoming what God has destined for you. Faith risks going beyond your comfort zone, desiring to know what God has for you out there.

And one more thing…

In Matthew 14:29, Jesus tells Peter to come to Him by walking on the water. He is 'daring' Peter to live life afraid. God knows that if Peter gives in to every fear he has, he will never accomplish what God has planned for him. Mighty men and women of God still have fear. But they have learned to tame it. They learn to bring every thought into captivity to the obedience of Christ (2 Corinthians 10:5). They say, "Here are my thoughts and fears today, Lord. What should I do with them?"

We sometimes think, "I wish I knew the future. If only I knew what would happen, I wouldn't be so scared!" But it's not true. If God showed us all He has planned for us, we would be overwhelmed. We would discount His plan as being way too risky. And we would rewrite our future. We have to factor in His grace for every situation. A former youth mentor, Bill Gotthard, described grace as "the desire and the power to do God's will." But remember, His grace is already at work in you. Often our desire to rely upon it arrives just when we need it.

So let's face it… sharing our faith is risky. It can be nerve-wracking and totally uncomfortable. But so can drowning. What do I mean? Well, when you learned to swim, you ran the serious possibility of drowning. But you calculated the risk, compared it to the success factor of others, and then you decided it was worth the risk. But without risk, there is no reward. Or as this generation says it, "No pain… no gain."

The things you can do for God without His help are few and boring. But the heights He is calling you to rise to definitely require His assistance, and your willingness to face and conquer your fears. God is calling you and I to step out of our comfort zone.

Go ahead. You'll be glad you did. Do it afraid.

It's scary fun!

Question to ponder:
With "10" being the highest and "1" being the lowest, what degree does fear play a role in my life and my witness? What level would I like it to be at?

Action point:
Why don't you pray a prayer something like this right now:

"Dear Lord,
You know me the best. You know what fears humans face. Would you increase Your compassion in my heart so it is larger than my fears? Help me to recognize and obey Your voice more than any other. I thank You my fears do not need to rule me anymore. In Jesus' mighty name I pray, amen."

4

THE REAL REASONS I DON'T SHARE MY FAITH

Testimony to remember:

I was in the airport in Delhi, India, and our flight was delayed for a few hours. We were tired and ready to return home. As we strolled through the airport, I decided I would share my faith regardless of how I felt. And to my surprise, we had the privilege of sharing our faith with three Hindu people, two of whom prayed right then to make Jesus their Lord. God taught me not to let my feelings rule me.

I once heard a story about a king who was looking for a husband for his only daughter. Only the bravest man in his kingdom would be worthy of marrying his beautiful daughter. So one day he assembled all the eligible bachelors and lined them up around his castle. Surrounding the castle was a big ditch filled with water and man-eating alligators. He set forth the terms of his contest to the men.

Whoever would be the first man to dive into the moat and safely swim to the other side would be the bravest man in his kingdom, and would win the hand of his daughter in marriage. As soon as the king had finished speaking, everyone heard a loud splash. They looked to find a young man already in the water. He was swimming with all his might, flailing his arms wildly, while frantically kicking off the alligators. He zig-zagged across the moat until he finally reached the other side safely. The king ran up to him with eagerness and congratulated him on being the bravest man. He joyfully said, "You can now marry my daughter. Is there anything you would like to say?"

The exhausted man said, "Yes, my king, there is something I would like to say. Who pushed me?"
Yes, sometimes King God pushes us into areas outside our comfort zone. God likes to 'stretch' us, because He knows we will grow stronger in Him. Will you allow the Holy Spirit to push you closer to the people He loves? Will you allow Him to stretch you today?

Let me be candid. I have missed many more opportunities to share my faith than I have taken. I'm such a wimp. Of what am I afraid? I'm not afraid of slalom water skiing, traveling to foreign countries, trying new foods, or confronting difficult issues. I'm not fearful of public speaking, death or even visiting the dentist.

So why don't I share my faith like I want? And why do I rationalize away my fears instead of just being candid and truthful with myself? Why do I fear what people will think of me?

I can come up with many clever reasons for not sharing my faith:
"I'm not ready."
"I cant' relate to him."
"I don't know what to say..." or the big one,
"I don't feel led."

If that doesn't resonate, how about these?
"I'm too busy."
"I'm in a hurry," or
"I'm afraid I will mess it up."

If those don't fit, it won't take my flesh long to custom-tailor another excuse.

"Sorry God, maybe I'll never get this right. Maybe the human race was not such a good pick to represent You."
Then again, maybe God meant to choose us... now that's sobering! So my friend, what are the real reasons for not sharing our faith? Are we daring and secure enough to actually talk about them? They are numerous, but let's go ahead and list some... with fear and trepidation. For some of us, this may be harder than going to the dentist's office. But let's do it anyhow. And let's "Do it afraid!" In fact, to help you out, I will go first. Here's my list.

SEVEN REAL REASONS I DON'T SHARE MY FAITH... REALLY:

1. MY FIRST LOVE IS FADING - I'll be honest. Sometimes my passion for Jesus wanes. My spiritual growth has at times been stunted, my intimate times in His presence are few, and the expectant joy of knowing and serving Him has been swallowed by the cares of life. I feel better now that I've said it.

2. FEAR - Fear of failure, of rejection, of not knowing what to say, of saying the wrong thing, of my mind going blank, of offending people and worrying about my reputation. Are you thinking by now that I have multiple issues?

3. APATHY - Little compassion, little concern about others, not <u>really</u> believing in an eternal Hell or Heaven, focusing mainly on myself by buying into our humanistic culture that says life is all about me and my happiness. Wow, this is worse than I wanted you to know.

4. BUSYNESS - Preoccupation with non-eternal issues, "loving things" and "using people" rather than the opposite, addicted to a full calendar because we feel better about ourselves, unable to handle down-time, etc. Guilty as charged.

5. PROCRASTINATION - Putting off until tomorrow what should rivet our attention today, hoping someone else will reach my neighbor, convincing myself there is no urgency. I guess if I procrastinate long enough, the urgency leaves, like an unwelcome guest.

6. A CRITICAL SPIRIT - Thinking *my* way is the only good way to reach people, minimizing others because their way is different than mine, or jealousy over other's success.
I can see where the enemy has distracted us from our real mission.

7. SPIRITUAL PRIDE - Thinking my time is wasted because all converts don't become mature disciples, thinking I don't have the gifts or commission to reach the unsaved, and impatience with the slow growth and immaturity of some. Maybe this is the biggest hindrance of all. Maybe it's time to humble myself.

Well, that was tough, but good for me. I have seen most of those in my own life at one time or another. Do any of those ring true with you? I'm guessing they do. Aren't you glad we have a patient Heavenly Father?

Let's face it... we may miss way more opportunities than we take. And yet God still chooses us to be His ambassadors... unbelievable! If I was God, some days I wouldn't choose myself! Yet God did choose a fearful Queen Esther, a prideful Samson, and a weary Moses. He deliberately chose impetuous Peter, a formerly demon-tormented man and a Christian-hater turned Christ-lover named Paul. And He chooses imperfect people like you and I to represent His perfect love! God chooses ordinary people to accomplish extraordinary things. For better or worse, you and I are part of His team.

In 2005, Liberia ended a brutal 14 year civil war. When I conducted crusades there in 2009, there was virtually no electricity for this entire African nation. Everything was completely dark at night, except for generator-driven lights. I am told the rebels flippantly destroyed the hydroelectric plants, thinking they could be easily repaired. But unfortunately the repair bill was over 300 million US dollars.

While flying out of Liberia, I noticed something that startled me. In my short time in Liberia, I had grown somewhat accustomed to dark cities at night, having to depend on a generator for any current I might need. But while flying out of the country and into Abidjan in the Ivory Coast, I was surprised to see a whole city lit up again at night.... as if this was something new to me!

The spiritual metaphor is both obvious and powerful. Christians are the light of the world. We are instructed not to hide our light under a bushel, thus bringing darkness. But we are to let it shine, illuminating all that is around us. God helps us to brighten our world. Our culture should be very happy for the Christians that are joyfully living their faith out-loud! Hiding our light only brings further darkness to our nations and our neighborhoods. Shining our light causes people to see their need, and thus come to know God's great forgiveness.

Listen to Jesus' thoughts in Matthew, "You are the light of the world. A city that is set on a hill cannot be hidden" (Matthew 5:14). So why isn't the church growing today? I was golfing one day with a Baptist pastor friend. I asked him the same question. He had an immediate and discerning response. Here's what he said:

WHY IS THE CHURCH NOT GROWING?

1. We lack intimacy with God.

    If we are not close to God's heart, we won't know what's dearest to Him. We are only close to the people with whom we spend time. Jesus said, "My sheep hear My voice" (John 10:27). If we will anticipate wonderful times in the Word and in prayer, we will reach intimacy with God. Tomorrow, approach your time with God with expectancy. You will be surprised what happens! And while you're on speaking terms with Him, ask Him to give you His heart for His people.

2. We are not "friends of sinners."

    If we don't rub shoulders with the lost, we cannot influence them. Jesus hung out with some of the worst... tax collectors and sinners. The religious people ridiculed Him for it. Before a fisherman can clean fish, he has to catch them. A mature disciple is involved in both catching and cleaning.

3. We assign evangelism to the professionals… pastors, evangelists and so on.

> We don't see evangelism as a responsibility and privilege of us all. Jesus' mandate to go into all the world applies to all Christians. Ephesians 4 says the pastoral offices are meant "for the equipping of the saints for the work of ministry" (Ephesians 4:11-12).

> All of us working together can make a huge difference! Synergy multiplies the church.

Let me add one more reason.

4. We have lost our sense of urgency.

> We act like we are going to live forever, and that we have plenty of time. As I am writing this, just yesterday a 26 year old local youth pastor was killed in a car accident in our town. We think we are guaranteed 70+ years, but we really don't know if we even have but one day left on earth. We must learn to redeem the time and make everyday count for eternal purposes. We must start now.

Well then, was that so hard? Some people never face their weaknesses. They're afraid. They stare at their excuses, only to be stared down. Isn't it refreshing to get our excuses out in the open? We then realize we are all in the same boat. Isn't it great that God doesn't condemn us for our weaknesses or fears?

The only way to successfully deal with our shortcomings is to pray over them, graciously talk about them with our friends, and act on them with God's strength. "PTA"… Pray, Talk, Act! Remember, Jesus said we are never alone. When we go, He goes with us… every time!

"Lo ["Yo" in modern language!], I am with you always, *even* to the end of the age." (Matthew 28:20)

Question to ponder:
What are the real reasons I don't share my faith?

_____
_____
_____

Action point:
Take the first step of no return across the line of your paralysis. Right now, tell God you are determined to defeat your excuses and be His witness.

5

HOW TO FALL IN LOVE... AGAIN!

Testimony to remember:
I was sitting in a horrifyingly hot Nigeria, Africa airport. An African man came to sit near me as I was drinking my Coke. It turned out he was raised in a Christian church, but left because he felt shunned. They had placed a black pew at the rear of the church where anyone who had not paid their tithes had to sit. I told him God did not want his money, but wanted his heart. I told him when his wife got engaged to him, it wasn't for his money. She wanted his heart. But when she got his heart, she got his money! That seemed to make a lot of sense to him. It's all about love from the heart. Later he came and found me on the airplane, and said, "I want to give my life back to Jesus Christ!" And right there, standing in the galley of our airplane flying 35,000 feet above the earth, he surrendered his life to Christ!

"But when He saw the multitudes, He was moved with compassion for them" (Matthew 9:36)

When I met Vicki, my wife-to-be, I was energized. Spending time with her was the highlight of my day. The sun and moon revolved around how often I could arrange to be with her. I was hopelessly in love. We would talk daily on the phone until 2 a.m., and then get up for work at 6 a.m. Then I would crash on the weekends and sleep in, but it was worth it. How could I relentlessly and tirelessly pursue this relationship? I was compelled by love.

It wasn't a sacrifice to be with her. No one had to twist my arm or suggest that I might want to see her soon. We could sit in a restaurant for hours talking about who-knows-what. It didn't matter. When we were together, life was fun. Her phone calls to me were not an interruption, but a delightful break from the routine of life. In fact, I didn't know how routine life was until I fell in love.

The reason I met my wife-to-be was I was already in love. You see, I wanted to hang out with college-age kids who were radically in love with Jesus like I was. So I sought them out, and eventually found my wife. These kids were so in love with the Lord that they would actually tell all their friends about Him. We started a church with fifty "Jesus Freaks," and it grew to 2,500 in twelve years. There was no evangelism program... just people in love!

Fast-forward a couple dozen years, and I am still hanging out with people who are hopelessly in love with Jesus. I love to share my faith with unbelievers, because every time I do, my fire for God reignites all over again. That's right... I come back to my first love whenever I share my story with pre-believers. Oh yes, it's scary at times, and risky. But what a blast! It is so fun to know that I have "the stuff" for which everyone is searching.

But there's a problem. Some of my friends who were so in love with Jesus have now bought into a hectic, busy lifestyle. Their love for Christ seems to have cooled down quite a bit. In fact, they rarely tell people about their love for Christ unless asked... which is never.

Their passion for God is cooling off. They feel guilty about not having the fire for God they once had, but seem unable to get out of the guilt-rut, and back onto Lover's Lane. They appear to be losing their first love. And if they would be candid, they would say they miss what they used to enjoy.

Then again, others who do share their faith seem to think *they* are the Holy Spirit. It's their job to make people feel guilty. Our dour, holier-than-thou faces are not the kind of advertisement God had in mind. Instead, we must be reminded the Bible says "that the goodness of God leads you to repentance" (Romans 2:4). Yes, people must see their sin before they see their need for a Savior. But we can lovingly show them we are all in the same boat... we have all done wrong, and our wrong separates us all from a holy God. We have to recapture the joy of knowing Jesus again in our own lives. Only then can we effectively and contagiously communicate it to others who are searching for true joy.

So, what should we do? Let's stop the car and get out. Get some fresh air and let's think this thing through. Is this what I signed up for when I received Christ? Was it really my intention to start the race hot and finish cold? What would I give to enjoy my faith again? Don't I want to break out of the "retirement" mode of Christianity? Do I want my life to pass from success to significance? If so, then this book is worth the read. It's time to enjoy your faith again!

Since we are being candid and upfront, here are some probing questions that will help us do a personal inventory:

> – Am I love-compelled or guilt driven?
> (What's my motive?)

– Am I in or out of love with Jesus?
(What would others say is my first love?)

– Is my spiritualk cup overflowing or almost empty?
(What's my current condition?)

So, how do I get my fire back? How do I change the past?

By falling in love again.

In my opinion, I find two primary ways that help me return to my first love… worship and evangelism.

1. Worship is intimate and exciting!

You were actually made to be a worshiper. Nothing else will fulfill you. Worship is the fulfillment of the greatest and first commandment that Jesus gave us—"*love the* L ORD *your God with all your heart, with all your soul, and with all your mind*" (Matthew 22:37). Worship is all about relationship! I connect in worship through times of praise, prayer and meditating on the Bible.

When I move beyond my feelings or circumstances, and choose to worship Him with all my heart, it's only a matter of time before His presence consumes me again, and His holy fire is ignited within me. We all have a God-shaped void in our lives, and only His presence can fill it. When I meditate on His word, and humble myself in a moment of prayer, His presence ignites in me all over again! It's the late night times when no one else is around, that I can pour out my heart to Him. It's the times when I sing to the Lord while driving my car, or as I read and re-read the Word slowly that holy goosebumps appear!

Listen to Psalm 16:11: "In Your presence *is* fullness of joy; At Your right hand *are* pleasures forevermore." The good news is I can learn to literally live in His presence. The ups and downs of life can be immediately submitted to His lordship in my life. I don't have to worry, hold a grudge, hate, have self-pity or give in to temptation. I don't have to yield to my fleshly and soulish leanings. I can walk in the Holy Spirit.

From my years of pastoring, I know I didn't always feel like preaching, worshipping, or even coming to church. But, I was the pastor, and didn't have a choice. So I chose to worship when I didn't feel like it. In my heart I said, "OK God, this is for you. I am going to worship by faith and as an act of honor to You." And do you know what happened? Every time, without fail, the presence of the Lord overwhelmed me and I felt refreshed! Why? Because I yielded to His Spirit rather than yielding to my flesh.

Worship will ignite your fire all over again... I guarantee it. Go ahead, put down the book for a few minutes and just start thanking God for all of His goodness to you.

2. Evangelism keeps us from getting stuffy and old.
It keeps us fresh, vibrant and relevant. Evangelism is the fulfillment of the second greatest commandment Jesus gave us—"*love your neighbor as yourself*" (Matthew 22:39). Most Christians who are losing their first love for Christ have stopped being Christ's hands and voice. When I move beyond my self I find great

opportunity to mature myself to become more Christ-like. If I mainly focus on my needs, then I quickly become a Dead Sea where there is inflow but no outflow. New life quickly is suffocated.

Have you ever been around a mom and her newborn baby? She quickly forgets the hardship and pain, but now holds the joy of her life. In the same sense, the happiest Christians I know are those who are helping others find the love of Christ! In fact, every time they share their faith, the fire of their joy gets ignited all over again.

Listen to how the psalmist David got his joy back in Psalm 51:10-13.

Worship - "Create in me a clean heart, O God, And renew a steadfast spirit within me. Do not cast me away from Your presence, And do not take Your Holy Spirit from me. Restore to me the joy of Your salvation, and uphold me *by Your* generous Spirit."

Evangelism - "*Then* I will teach transgressors Your ways, And sinners shall be converted to You."

Even David had lost his joy through his own decisions to follow his flesh rather than God's Spirit. But now he is making spiritual decisions that will ignite his fire all over again, and prepare him for years of fruitful ministry as God had planned.

My friend, what do we have to lose but our boring approach to God? Let's ask God to restore and increase our joy again. Let's start having fun living for Jesus without limits. Total abandonment... that's what will bring incredible joy! Let's fall in love... again!

It was 1996, and I was at a historic conference in Atlanta, Georgia where 40,000 clergy were gathered for a Christian men's conference called Promise Keepers. The RCA domed stadium was simply electric with the energy of thousands of men singing praise to God!

Little did I know that this day was to change my life, and the lives of thousands... forever.

One speaker told us to turn around and introduce ourselves to someone behind us and ask Him one question... "How did you come to know Christ as your Savior?" The man I talked to was pastor Ermilio from Asuncion, Paraguay in South America. He began to tell his awesome story.

He said before he came to Christ, he was training six hours per day for the Paraguayan Olympic games. After he found Christ, God prompted him to give himself to prayer with the same intensity he had done for the Olympic games.

He started a church in the living room of his home with ten people, a tattered tambourine and a broken accordion. And still he prayed six hours per day. And now he was at this domed stadium looking for structural ideas for their new church building, for they now had 6,000 people attending their church services.

And God spoke to my heart right then. He told me... "Tom, go home and double your prayer time. Seek My face, and not My hand."

It was not that so much prayer equaled such church growth, but I knew God was calling me to a deeper level of relationship with Him! I knew it was good and even scriptural to ask God for things, but I sensed God was inviting me into a higher realm of worship.

So for the next 30 days I tried not to ask God for anything. It was very hard, for I was a pastor, and there are always many needs to bring before God. But for this season, I tried to only worship Him! I doubled my prayer time, and grew to love my time with Him more than ever. It was a challenge, but after 30 days, something amazing took place. In one week's time, I had not one, but two different invitations to travel abroad and conduct outdoor evangelistic meetings. One invitation came from India, and the other from Africa. Now understand, God brought these men to me. I did nothing to solicit their invites. I lived in Minneapolis, and rarely received an invitation to speak ten miles away in Saint Paul, much less internationally. Who was I to get such invitations? As I was falling in love with Him on a deeper level, God's favor was opening new doors of opportunity.

This was an answer to my prayers as a 12 year old boy. I sensed at a young age God had called me to be an evangelist that would win masses of people to Christ. In fact, after seeing Billy Graham at one of his crusades, I wrote him and told him of my calling.

And Psalm 37:4 became my *life-verse...* "Delight yourself also in the LORD, and He shall give you the desires of your heart."

I found the closer I got to God's heart, my desires started changing and purifying. And the closer I got to His heart, the less I was striving in my own flesh to try to accomplish something for God. Now I was leaving the strategy and timing up to His discretion.

It's a great feeling to be free from striving to accomplish something for God. It is freeing just to be in His presence, knowing my worth comes from Him and not from what I do for Him.

The more I worship, the more He pours out His favor on my life.

When I had little kids, they would tug on my pant legs and say "Daddy, Daddy! Give me, give me... help me, help me."

But now I have some young granddaughters. And when they see me coming, they run to me and jump up in my arms, and give me a kiss on the cheek. They aren't asking for anything. They just came to show their love to me.

And what does grandpa do? He reaches in his pocket and says, "Let's go buy some ice cream! Let's go buy you a new dress!" Why? Because favor follows love. And I think this is what God is like. When I love him with all my heart with a childlike faith, He reaches in His pocket and begins to pour out His favor on me. In fact, I believe that God's favor can do in 6 minutes what it takes me 6 years to accomplish. Go ahead, delight yourself in the Lord, and see what happens!

Question to ponder:
When I pray, do I usually seek His face more than His hand?

Action point:
When you pray and read the Bible today, ask God to speak to you personally... today!

6

NO LONGER A SPECTATOR

Story to remember:

I heard about a 5 year old girl that was lost in a massive cornfield in a USA rural town. The corn can grow taller than a grown man in height, making it impossible for this little girl to know where she was, or have any sense of direction. How would she find her way out, and how would her parents find her? Instead of panicking, the parents spread the word through their small town that a member of their community was lost. The townspeople eagerly rallied behind the parents. They had a strategy they knew would work. They formed a single-file line of people the length of the entire cornfield, and walked through it hand-in-hand until someone finally found the girl!

It's simple, yet profound. When we are motivated by love, we will always find a way. Love moves us from being spectators to being participants.

You may have heard of the analogy that describes a typical

professional football game at the sports stadium:

> "Twenty-two athletes on the field desperately in need of rest, being coached by 60,000 thousand fans desperately in need of exercise!"

As funny as it seems, we know it's easy to be an armchair-quarterback. We cheer when our team is winning, and we rant and rave when they make mistakes. Surely we could do as well as them!

As a pastor for many years, I sometimes set the wrong example. By default, I got a lot of my worth from accomplishing tasks before me on my desk. It seemed like an endless stream of attention-grabbing emails, letters, appointments, studying and things to put on my to-do list. But sometimes it kept me so busy at my desk doing good things, that our neighborhoods went largely unreached. Worse yet, I contributed to the model of what we know as "spectator Christianity": a crowd of people sitting on the pews soaking up the continuous teaching with little or no application expected.

I am told approximately 70% of college age young adults stop going to church. Why? That's a great question. I think part of the answer is that they are tired of being a spectator. They want front-line, meaningful encounters that will stretch their faith and give aid to others in need. They want to get off the bleachers and into the game. Teaching without application makes us "know-it-all spectators." It's not enough to just sit in the pew, or to just have a holy huddle, as if we we're going to play in the game. The preparation is all intended for the action of the game.

So here's my point…
Knowledge without application is useless. (Would you read that again, please?)

Church is supposed to be all about relationships: with Christ, with each other, and with those yet to be reached. All three are needed to be healthy.

> **– Relationship with Christ**... this is hands-down the most exciting journey ever offered to the human race. I get the opportunity of communicating with the God who made it all happen.. the earth, the universe, the embryo, the heart, and everything else. This majestic God wants to talk to me! And the more I seek to communicate with Him, the more He wants to show me His love…His grace… His glory… and His utter and indescribable, magnificent presence! This is way too good to be true.

> **– Relationship with each other**... friendship is one of the greatest gifts God gives us. And when we become Christians, we immediately inherit a zillion other "brothers, sisters, fathers and mothers" in the faith. We become part of the heavenly family that will never cease to exist. I know we have all had our squabbles with a few. We wish everyone could just be a little more like us. But God made us each in His image, and we glorify Him when we are patient and when we love one another.

> **– Relationship with those yet to know Christ**... I love John 17:20. "I do not pray for these alone, but also for those who will believe in Me through their word." It is really the Lord's prayer as He prays not only for those who are following Him now, but He prays for those yet to know him! This is exciting because it means heaven's gates are still open. There is still more

room for your unsaved family members, friends and neighbors. Judgment is coming, but His mercy is still available to the worst of sinners, or the best of sinners. Jesus is praying for your family!

This last point is the main focus of this book... those *yet* to know Christ. When we try to reach others for Christ, the first two get healthier also. I am made to be a conduit, not a container. When Christ flows through me to others, I begin to feel more compassion for the human race, and I also am drawn closer to my Lord Jesus as His unconditional love flows through me.

This is a "win-win-win" for every Christian. When we reach out to others, we're drawn closer to others God loves, and thus closer to God. We can't lose!

My friend Craig told me, "Jesus never said 'if you build it they will come.'" He always went to the people, where they were. The New Testament church was organic."

For example, I stopped at a gas super-station while out of town. Upon entering the store I saw what appeared to be a homeless man sitting on a picnic table outside, smoking a cigarette with a couple knapsacks next to him. Upon returning to my car, I decided to engage him in conversation, and asked if he had eaten recently. He hadn't, so I offered to buy him a sandwich. As we talked, I realized he wasn't what I had thought he would be. He had a story, a family, some hard times and was all alone. After chatting a while, I turned the conversation to the Lord. He perked up, and said he actually had a Bible in his knapsack, but hadn't found the courage to give His life to Jesus. He went on to tell me of a vision God had given him while homeless of a perfectly white robe. I told him this was probably God telling him that God offers to forgive him and make him perfectly clean, and to clothe him with His love.

He always thought he had to clean up his life first, and then come to God. But I had the awesome privilege of telling him that only Christ can clean us up, and we come to Him just as we are. It seemed to make sense to him. So we prayed right there at that picnic table for him to finally surrender his life to Christ. I offered to pick him up at the same spot to go to church the next day. He agreed. I said, "OK, 9:30 a.m. right here tomorrow morning." I have been disappointed in the past, as we all have. Sometimes people agree to join us and then don't show up. But I didn't doubt he would be there.

Sure enough, he was there waiting as I drove into the lot. We went to church, and he asked me, "Where should we sit?" I told him I didn't care, so he brought us up to the very front row. So here I was, sitting in a new church front and center with a homeless man who had just received Jesus, and I thought this was pretty good. When the offering came, I threw in a few bucks to be a good example, but he dug in his pockets and emptied them... about 83 cents. I knew right away who had given more.

At the end of our lunch together, I was so glad I had opened my heart to let God love through me. It wasn't a burden, but a blessing... for both of us. He had made some new contacts, and I had new love pouring into my heart to replace that which I had used. In fact, I think I was more blessed than him.

Questions to ponder:

On a scale of 1-10, with 10 being the highest, how would other people that know me rate my love for Christ? My love for each other? My love for those yet to know Christ?

#_____

Action point:

Decide now what number you would like to be rated at 90 days from now. #_____

Decide what I need to do to get to that number.

_____

7

CHANGE MY HEART, OH GOD

Quote to remember:
"I think 90% of Christians live with the guilt of evangelism."
~Pastor Steve Nickel

My wife and I were flying back from an awesome trip to Israel. As I saw the places where Jesus walked, my heart was stirred again with a new resolve to share my faith even more. I was determined to change and be His witness more faithfully.

I was in the airplane restroom thinking about my desire to share my faith. (It's strange where the Holy Spirit chooses to speak to you!) But upon exiting the restroom, I saw the flight attendant sitting in the back of the plane reading a magazine. The thought came to me, "Share your faith with her." Now I have come to learn this is often how the Spirit leads us. When we are living our daily lives, and suddenly this desire to share with someone comes; I should simply obey. I don't have to know why.

So I began to talk to her. When I told her we had been in Israel, she mentioned her desire to one day visit it herself. I asked if she would like to see some of my photos of Israel. She was eager, so I went back to my seat and retrieved my camera. I began to show her many photos. But while sharing, another flight attendant started looking at them also. So now there's three of us standing in the rear galley of the plane, and I am wondering what God is up to.

I began to share how exciting it was to walk in the Holy Land, my best experience was when the Holy Land started becoming real to me. I asked if I could visit with them about it, and they were all ears. So I shared my *ONE MINUTE WITNESS* with them.

When I was done, I asked if they had any spiritual beliefs, and asked if they thought they were ready to go to heaven one day. They were not sure, so I took it to the next step.

I asked if I could share how the Bible says they can know they are going to heaven when they die. They were still eager, so I continued on, aware that God was keeping them from being interrupted. I shared the ABCs. It goes like this:

A. **Admit** I have done wrong. We have all done wrong, haven't we? And if heaven is perfect, then none of us can enter. So we all have a big problem.

B. **Believe** that only Jesus Christ dying for my wrong can remove my sin. And by rising from the dead, He proved He was really God. Since my good works cannot erase my bad works, I really need someone to help me.

C. **Confess** my sins to God and ask His forgiveness. I ask Jesus to be the Lord of my life. The word "Lord" means "boss" or "owner" of my life. I must ask Jesus to be the leader of my life everyday.

I then asked them if they understood what I had just presented to them. They both said yes. So I asked them a key question:

"What would hold you back from surrendering your life to Jesus right now?"

Both of them said nothing would prevent them. So I held out my hand, and asked if I could pray with them to receive Jesus into their lives. And to my joyful surprise, they both placed their hand into my open hand!

And we prayed a sinner's prayer. Three of us were standing in the back of the plane by God's design, and all heaven was listening.

At the end, the first woman said, "It's so exciting you talked to us today. You see, today is the one year anniversary of my mother passing away. Just this morning I asked God to send me some sort of encouragement on this very difficult day. I am so grateful He sent you."

Of course, I was flying so high I didn't need the airplane to get home. Wow! What a fun thing it was to offer myself available to the Lord, and then see such a great response. Here's the key: I had to make myself available to be used. It was up to me to change.

I became God's mouthpiece. This is my continual challenge. Will I be available again today? Or will my busyness crowd out these potential divine appointments? I probably miss many more than I yield to, but my goal is different now.

After 20 years of being a senior pastor, here is one of the major lessons I learned:

I can't make people change!

Yes, I can influence them. You can lead a horse to the water, but you can't make him drink. The only one I can truly change is *me*.

The late great preacher Charles Spurgeon says there is really only one sin. He says every other sin we commit finds its roots in this one sin... pride. With what sins do we struggle? Hatred, bitterness, lust, greed, and jealousy... to name a few. Pride is all about me, me, me.

When Lucifer was an angel in God's glorious heaven, pride entered his heart. He said, "I will be like the Most High" (Isaiah 14:14).

When someone hurts or offends us, our tendency is to retaliate openly or inwardly.

Pride causes men to see women as objects of our lust. Pride causes us to have an insatiable appetite for that which can never really satisfy. Pride tells us I deserve better, and I always need more.

Pride also keeps us from loving people the way Jesus did. It puts me first. It marginalizes other people and their needs, and elevates my perceived needs.

Could this be one key reason we don't share our faith like we ought? Are we like those religious men who passed by the wounded man, only to see the lowly and despised Samaritan stop and give aid to the one in need? Does pride tell us we are way too busy or not confident enough to share our faith? Is pride the root of our fear of rejection? Does it keep us from reaching out to our neighbors and workmates, fearing what they will think of us?

Let's be candid. This whole idea of surrendering all and dying to myself is intriguing. I have asked myself, "Are these just trite Christian phrases I banter about, or is this my heart's true prayer?"

If I respond authentically, I have to admit my dying-to-self days are not yet finished. I understand more clearly why the apostle Paul says, "I die daily." This must be my continuous goal.

So clearly we realize we only have a faith worth sharing when we invite the Holy Spirit to change us from the inside out. Anything less is not worth replicating in others. Jesus spoke of Himself once when he said, "learn from Me, for I am gentle and lowly in heart, and you will find rest for your souls" (Matthew 11:29).

Life wasn't about him, but about pleasing His father. His mission was clear… "to seek and to save that which was lost" (Luke 19:10).

He had no PR person, and no slick ads. His promotion came from the signs and wonders He did, which came from humbly being in the presence of His father God.

So how can I care like Jesus cared? I must ask Him to change my heart to be like His... every day.

Since Jesus was tempted in every way we are, it means He was tempted to be apathetic, uncaring, selfish, and prideful. He was tempted to look down on people, to run His own daily agenda rather than God's, and to grow weary of trying to help people who were full of themselves. He was tempted to let the burdens of life wear Him down to the point he felt He had nothing left to give to others.

But we know that He did not succumb. Why? He was anointed and filled with pride's opposite spirit... *humility*. His whole life was about dying… from the manger to Calvary. He left heaven, knowing He was equal to God, yet humbled Himself by becoming a man. He called out the religious pride of the Pharisees, while keeping his heart tender to those whom He was called to reach. He kept prayer his number one priority, knowing that He, as a man, desperately needed daily strength to resist His own prideful potential. In the wilderness He defeated the devil's arrogance with humility and truth. And even while dying on the cross, he sang a song of forgiveness as prophesied in Psalm 22.

And so, we too must sing a song of confession made popular by Vineyard:

> "Change my heart oh God, make it ever true.
> Change my heart oh God, may I be like You…"

There is only one king for every throne… one driver for every car… one head for every body…and one God for every heart. Today I again have the choice of jumping back in the driver's seat of my own life, or giving the keys again to Jesus and inviting Him to drive my life.

My pride is absolutely ugly, and it makes sharing my faith routine and loveless. If I don't embrace humility, I will begin to eventually despise the very ones I am sent to reach. Moses did so in a fit of rage as he was fed up with the complaining and whining of the children of Israel. He hit the rock to bring forth drinking water for the people instead of speaking to it as God commanded. He shouted at the people, "Must we bring water for you out of this rock?" (Numbers 20:10). He was burned out because he was not refreshed. My heart naturally grows hard to others' needs unless I ask God to daily refresh my heart to be like His.

Let's do it before it's too late.

Question to ponder:

What two things tend to draw my heart away from my love for Christ?

_____

_____

Action point:

Before you go to bed tonight, will you find a place to bow your heart before God and ask Him to change you? Maybe you want to stop reading right now and slowly breathe a prayer from your heart like this:

> *"Dear God,*
> *Today I rejoice that I am Your child... completely*
> *forgiven, eternally blessed, and unconditionally loved.*
> *I've been promised the sweet assurance of heaven.*
>
> *But I have neglected what you love most... people.*
> *Please forgive me for my sinful and selfish pride.*
> *Change my heart to weep for what You weep, and to love*
> *the way You love. Give me the discernment and will to*
> *avoid the temptations of my selfish flesh. I confess my*
> *total dependence upon You and Your daily work in me.*
>
> *Remove my carnal heart desires, and replace them with*
> *the pure desires of heaven.*
>
> *Let me hear Your loving voice again, and help me*
> *extend that love to the lost as You do. Let me see every*
> *unreached person as someone for whom You died. Let*
> *me see the holy importance of their unsaved soul to You.*
> *I confess that their salvation is more serious to You than*
> *any other request I could make for myself.*
>
> *Now open my eyes to the wonderful gift of today.*
> *Let me invest this day in a way that will bring a smile to*
> *Your face, and fame to Your name instead of mine.*
>
> *In Jesus' most humble name I pray,*
> *Amen."*

8

A BIBLICAL MANDATE FOR TELLING YOUR STORY

Verse to remember:

"Go home to your friends, and tell them the great things the Lord has done for you" (Mark 5:19)

I love the power of before-and-after advertisements. "I used to be 340 pounds, but now since I used this battery-operated tummy-shaker once a month, I am down to 120 pounds!" Unbelievable! And yet people still buy the tummy-shaker. Or an Olympic gold-medal "look-alike" champion is working out on the exercise ball, saying, "if you roll on this ball for 20 minutes a day, you could look like me!" Unbelievable!

Why are we so gullible? Yet the power of a person's testimony sells billions of dollars of stuff we don't need and will never use.

But then there is Jared Fogle, a student at Indiana University that weighed 425 pounds. He decided to eat at Subway sandwich shops, and through a controlled diet and walking, lost 245 pounds in one year. Amazing... but true.

But what about a real, true-to-life testimony from someone you trust? Don't you listen more intently when you feel their story is authentic and personal? In fact, you have a story to tell too. Yes, you! But you may say, "I don't have much of a story... I wasn't a drug addict or alcoholic." But you have a story of a changed life that is true today. Your changed life will speak volumes to many people, whether their past is like yours or not.

Every human being has three things in common.

- First, we all need to be loved.

- Second, we all need to be accepted.

- Third, we all need to be needed.

Isn't that what Jesus gave you... love, acceptance and purpose? Yes! Oh, your story may be quite different from someone else's story, but we are all wired with the same basic needs. Only in Christ can these needs be fully met. No husband or wife nor money or education can fill the void in our lives that is God-shaped.

Look at Mark 5:1-20. This demon-possessed man was continually tormented. The demons would control him, causing him to cut himself deeply with sharp stones. The demonic power would break chains that bound him, and he would cry out all night with eerie, demonic, blood-curdling, guttural screams. He was a mess. He had no future...no hope... until one day Jesus walked by.

With one word from Jesus, his life was changed! The vast darkness that had tormented him for so long was now eclipsed by a holy light that flooded his mind. He was finally in his right mind. And he instinctively knew why. He, above all people, knew the origin of his torment. The difference he sensed was like stepping from a pitch-black room into a strong ray of sunlight. It was overwhelming, to say the least. He was forever grateful and even tried to follow Jesus to be with him, a heart-felt request from a man who had been completely transformed.

But Jesus had a different idea. However, Jesus wouldn't let him, but said to him, "Go home to your friends, and tell them what great things the Lord has done for you, and how He has had compassion on you."

"Wait a minute, Jesus! This man just wants to follow you. Isn't that what you want... followers? Now you want him to go back to his people and witness to them? Why, he doesn't know any memory verses from the Bible. He has never been through Evangelism Explosion. He doesn't know the Roman's Road. He doesn't have any gospel tracts to give to people. He has never even been to church. He is a baby believer. Aren't you expecting just a little too much?"

No. If you have been forgiven, you have a story to tell! If you have a Savior, your changed life is a sermon. A transformed life is Christianity's best advertisement. I once was lost, but now am found! You have a story to share!

We must encourage people upon coming to Christ to immediately share their story with their family and friends. It not only benefits the hearer and again ignites us, but it will defeat the plans of the enemy as they repeatedly share the change Christ has made in their heart. "And they overcame him by the blood of the Lamb and by the word of their testimony..." (Revelation 12:11).

Statistics tell us the average new believer in Christ loses contact with nearly all of his old friends within two years. Yet, Jesus wants our influence to be felt outside the church building. Signs and wonders were to display God's power to unbelievers. But we have sanitized the Gospel, and worse yet, sanitized the new believer. It's like we are carrying some sanitized towelettes with us to wash off the world's bacteria every time we go out of our Christian bubble. The Bible says we are to be in the world, but not of it. We've done OK with the last part, but we are failing miserably when it comes to being in the world. Salt was never made to remain in the shaker. It is only effective when it is dispensed.

Jonah was the reluctant evangelist, but he finally went to the sinful city of Nineveh. What happened? The city repented and judgment was averted. Wow!

The woman at the well was caught in a life of confusing choices. But when Jesus engaged her with His message, she brought the whole town to hear Him!

Andrew went and found his brother Simon, the fisherman, and brought him to the Lord. Simon in turn became 'Peter', and was one of the greatest disciples we know!

But here in Mark chapter five, is perhaps one of the most unique examples of God using anybody. This former demon-possessed man was quick to obey. He went to Decapolis, and told all that Jesus had done for him... and all people marveled!

You may not have such an extreme testimony that involves such a visible transformation. But you do have a changed life...

- You have new peace where there used to be stress.

- You have new joy that circumstances cannot rob.

- You have a new hope of going to heaven.

- You have God's promise that you will see your loved ones again in heaven if they knew Christ as Savior.

As a disciple of Jesus Christ, you and I now have a privilege and an assignment. In fact it is a heavenly mandate... "Go into all the world and preach the gospel to every creature" (Mark 16:15).

You have exactly what the world is looking for... love, acceptance and purpose! This book will now help you outline your own personal story. You will be able to politely share it over and over again. With this method, people will not turn you off or slam the door in your face. This evangelism tool will help you to easily share with your neighbors and friends in a manner that they will respect. After all, you are just telling your story. And you are sowing a seed of God's love for them as you speak.

Get ready to enjoy sharing your faith without fear. Your Christian life will never be the same again. Are you ready?

Question to ponder:
What will it take for me to move from a place of agreeing we are part of the Great Commission, to actually personally participating in it?

Action point:
Write down any excuses or reasons you could not share your faith personally. Try to find Biblical support for your reasons. Good luck!
_____.

9

A BIBLICAL WAY TO DUMP YOUR GUILT

Quote to remember:
Bill Bright, the founder of Campus Crusade for Christ, defined a successful witness as, *"Sharing the claims of Christ under the power of the Holy Spirit, and leaving the results to God."*

Let's get rid of some more guilt. We must be very clear on one very important point. It is God's will that we share our story. But it is God's job to save people.

I heard the story of a missionary who served in Burkino Faso, Africa, a very strong Muslim area. In two years of ministry he could only account for one, true, new disciple of Jesus Christ. I thought rather smugly to myself, "well, I would have certainly had better results than this." What a prideful thought! We need to define scriptural success in one word... obedience. We all have both times of sowing and reaping. But all times must be rooted in obedience. Jesus only did what the Father told Him to do. God is still patiently trying to teach me this all-important lesson. Paul said in 2 Corinthians 10:12 we are both unwise and unspiritual when we compare ourselves amongst ourselves, or measure our success by someone else's. In 1 Corinthians 4:2 he tells us how we will be judged... by our faithfulness... period. His one, new African disciple might bring thousands to Christ.

Why do we think we have to convert people or pressure them to pray a sinner's prayer in order to feel good about what we did? For me, this used to be huge. It seems I only really felt good about my witnessing encounter if I could pray a sinner's prayer with someone. If I didn't close the sale, I felt I could have done better. But this is not true. People generally are repulsed by spiritual hype. They know when we have gone from sharing our story, to using pressure tactics.

You see, we all know people don't usually come to Christ the first time they hear about His plan. In fact, I've heard the average person who comes to Christ has already heard the gospel 7 times. Is the fourth time just as important as the seventh? Of course it is.

So our job is simply to share the story of a God who loves them unconditionally. When we do our job, the Holy Spirit does His. He draws them to Jesus. In fact, no person has ever come to Christ without being wooed by the Holy Spirit. I cannot convict them of sin. That's the Holy Spirit's job. I can make them feel guilty. I can pressure them. I can hype the gospel and use condemnation. But those are not the ways the Holy Spirit uses. He is gentle ("the goodness of God leads you to repentance" Romans 2:4).

I think my motives used to get confused. I felt God was more pleased with me when I actually led them to Him in prayer. I think I even found some of my acceptance before the Lord from this.

That's simply wrong thinking! Let me say this loud and clear to anyone else who thinks like I did:

My acceptance from God was already proved at Calvary.

He does not love me any more or any less based on my behavior. Yes, I will build up rewards in heaven for faithful service... but that's just it. Faithfulness and humility are what God is looking for... not how many notches are on my soul-winning belt. My greatest delight is in knowing Him first, and secondly in serving Him faithfully and humbly. This alone is enough of a challenge for a lifetime. And if I obey Him fully, then I will have great fruit in heaven someday.

So, what about our motives? Can we be totally honest and candid with each other? I was talking to a church secretary about sharing our faith, and she was shockingly honest with me. She said, "I don't think I even care about where my neighbor will spend eternity." In my pride, I thought to myself, "she is not a very good Christian." But in truth, I have to admit that often I haven't cared about my own neighbors to the point of action. In fact, there's still some neighbors for whom I don't pray, and the ones for whom I do pray, I know I could pray for more. But when have I prayed enough? It comes back to faithfulness. I must pray and ask God to soften my heart, and then try to be faithful to pray for them as often as God places them in my mind or on my heart.

But what if I don't care that I don't care? What if my heart has grown cold to their true spiritual condition? What if, in all honesty, I have just seen them as another notch on my spiritual belt that will help me feel better about myself before God? What if they never find Christ? Do I care? I heard a solution to hard-heartedness that I love a lot: try tears.

Tears? When was the last time I asked God for tears?

My Dad was a weeper. He is now in heaven, but when he was here he was one godly man. When he prayed, he wept. He could pray over a chicken sandwich, and before he was done his voice was cracking, thanking God for much more than the sandwich. His heart was tender... and compassionate. I have often asked God to let me have my Dad's tears. What a legacy to leave behind!

Jesus wept. Yes, I know it's the shortest scripture in the whole Bible, but it's true. Listen to Matthew 9:36: "But when He saw the multitudes, He was moved with compassion for them, because they were weary and scattered, like sheep having no shepherd." In the Greek, "moved with compassion" refers to having a major stomach ache. It's a miserable feeling.
We don't relate with this shepherd/sheep talk. But in Bible times they did. In fact, when I drive in India, I regularly see a flock of sheep or goats walking down the road or in the valley. But they are never without a shepherd. The shepherd-boy might only be eight years old, but they feel guided and protected. But if he thought his sheep might be unprotected and vulnerable to a wolf's attack, it would break his heart. He would worry non-stop about his sheep.

How much more does God, the Father, care about his sheep? He weeps over those who are so vulnerable to the lies of the devil. As He watches His creation being abused, He can still remember the day He turned His eyes away from His sin-laden Son on the cross. God still weeps tears of love for all His lost sheep today.

David said something profound about tears. Listen to Psalm 126:4-6, as he describes the tears that Israel felt as they lived in bondage to their enemies. "Bring back our captivity, O LORD, As the streams in the South. Those who sow in tears Shall reap in joy. He who continually goes forth weeping, Bearing seed for sowing, Shall doubtless come again with rejoicing, Bringing his sheaves *with him*."

This is God's cure for a hard heart... tears. Ask God to see people's eternal destiny. Ask God to let you see your neighbor through His eyes. Ask God what He sees and how He feels about the unsaved near your home. I have found that tears don't flow easily for me. I have also found my heart is harder that I would like to admit. I used to pray, "God, send sinners to my church." Now I pray, "God, I'm available today to go to them where they are. Put fresh compassion in me." Tears moisturize and soften even the hardest of hearts! Try tears.

When my tears are more than my fears, compassion wins every time. A soft and caring heart will help me lead many more to Christ. If I want to win one person to Christ each month, I will share my story many more times before I find the one that is truly ready. But it truly is the Lord who softens hearts. I will tell you what will increase your odds greatly. Pray that God will lead you daily to someone who is open and searching... whose heart is tender, and maybe even wounded. Pray that God will give you an understanding heart to feel empathy with them in their pains of life. That's the kind of heart King Solomon prayed for when he first became king.

The other thing we must realize is each person is at a different level of spiritual searching and readiness. If I pressure them to pray, so I can get another notch on my soul-winning belt, the fruit may not remain.

Let's just enjoy sharing our story... and let God do the saving. You will see it in their eyes if they are ready to hear more than your story. Many will be ready to hear more, and you can ask them if they would like to know this great joy too!

But that's not all. Every time you share your story from your heart, your own first-love fire will ignite within you all over again! I guarantee it.

Questions to ponder:
Alexander Maclaren was quoted as saying, "You tell me the depth of a Christian's compassion, and I will tell you the measure of his usefulness."

Do you suffer from the guilt of evangelism? Are you driven more by guilt or by compassion?

Action point:
Write the word "compassion" on a piece of paper and tape it to your mirror. For the next two weeks, pray for a dose of fresh compassion every morning before you start your day.

10

A BIBLICAL INVITATION TO "GO"

Quote to remember:
"We must motivate the church to get out of the seats and into the streets." ~Ted Lyke

In 1906 a horseback-riding evangelist came to a little town in northern USA called Lake Bronson, Minnesota. It's near the USA-Canadian border. He conducted some gospel meetings in a home. Everyone was excited to attend. The Spirit of God filled those meetings with His power and presence.

And someone invited the town drunk.

And the town drunk attended.

He heard the good news of the gospel, and he gave his life to Christ. As he grew in the Lord, he threw away his alcohol and snuff, and stopped beating his wife. His devotion to the Lord was so passionate, he became known in Lake Bronson as "a trumpet for God."

His 16-year-old grandson, Allard, came to visit him for the summer. He saw the radical change in his grandpa, and decided to rededicate his life to Christ. As Allard grew strong in his faith, he joined the US Army. Upon leaving the Army, he found a godly and beautiful woman named Ruth. Together they raised four children to love the Lord with a holy passion like theirs.

And I am one of the four children.

Yes, Al and Ruth Elie were my wonderful parents. And the town drunk was my great-grandpa Evenson!

Someday when I get to heaven, I am going to thank that horseback-riding evangelist. But I especially want to find the one who dared to invite the town drunk to their meetings. I want to personally say "thank you for caring!"

So you are reading this book because someone invited the town drunk to Jesus! Remember, nothing happens... until somebody cares.

You and I have a choice. Go or stay. Speak or be silent. Obey or ignore. Eternal lives are in the balance, earnestly longing for someone to show them the way. Evangelist Bill Fay encourages us to "capture the moment God creates."

Once there was an imaginary man named Joe Schmo. Joe is the average church-going, occasionally-involved, sometimes-praying and obeying, God-loving Christian. He wants to make a difference in his world, but to be perfectly honest, has a hard time reconciling his godly desires with what he actually sees in his own life. How can he help others when his own life often seems messed up? Furthermore, he doesn't think he is that different from most people he sees in the church. In fact, when he gets around evangelistic-type people, his rationalizer kicks in quickly, because he is easily overwhelmed.

Listen to his thoughts as he processes last Sunday's sermon about reaching his world for Christ.

> Pastor: "The Mandate? YOU... go into all the world.. and preach the gospel... to every creature. Period." (Matthew 28).

> Joe: "Sounds pretty heavy to me. I have enough stress in my life already. Plus, I'm not the evangelistic type... whatever that is."

> Pastor: "The Message? A perfect God wants an imperfect people to share an awesome life with Him. He is the only God of any religion who personally offered the ultimate demonstration of His love. He is crazy about His creation, and love-sick in His heart. He hurts when we hurt, and parties when we discover His real love."

> Joe thinks: "I can buy into this. The world has been looking for love forever, and Christ seems to have the solutions. I sure know I haven't found anything better."

> Pastor: "The Medium? You guessed it... us!"

Joe's thoughts: "God, you've got to be kidding. I wouldn't have chosen me… nor probably any other human. Angels would have certainly been a more humble and reliable spokespeople. But you had to choose us. Bummer!"

Pastor: "The Method? God wants us to be creative in using methods our world respects to reach people where they are. The methods change, but the message always stays the same."

Joe's thoughts: "Now I feel overwhelmed. Yet, maybe our approach could use some updating. If someone could show me how to talk normal to my neighbor about my faith in Christ without getting flaky, I definitely would be interested. But where do I start?"

Do Joe's thoughts seem reasonable? Do you relate at all with him? I sure do.

We have all had times when we don't feel good enough to be God's mouthpiece. And we have all dealt with the fear of rejection. But here's the point. God chose us, you and I, to be the imperfect messengers of a perfect gospel.

I'm not very witty or intellectual. I think most people aren't. If I have a few minutes to think about what I am going to write or speak, I may be halfway interesting. But God, the maximum-creativity God, wants to use our humble, stuttering voices to declare His holy and loving intentions to our world. Like Moses said when God told him to speak to Egypt's Pharaoh, we echo… *"Who, me?"* (Exodus 3:11 paraphrased).

Why not? Why shouldn't we take this assignment much more seriously than anything else? Of what are we afraid? Rejection, fear of failure, not knowing what to say and when to say it are all common excuses. But if we are God's "A" team, why are we satisfied with giving God excuses for not doing our homework?

Most days I consider myself a relatively mature follower of Christ...don't you?

But shouldn't there be a time in all of our maturing as disciples that we see through the empty reasons we use to justify our lack of fruitfulness? Why can't we just be honest with God? (Remember: He doesn't love us any more or less based on our performance.) Let's face reality...we're often missing the boat when it comes to reaching our world. In fact, we aren't even near the dock much of the time.

I am told over the last ten years, the church in the USA has had almost no positive net church growth. The Northwest USA area only has 2% of the population that attends any kind of church regularly. Hindu India has a higher percentage of evangelical Christians than Seattle. And worst of all, much of the church at large doesn't seem to care. Apathy is strangling the average church. Many pastors seem to be reluctantly following the current, rather than leading by swimming upstream. The more we ignore the great commission of Christ, the more nominal the church will become.

Feel the need yet?

Enough then. Let's ask God for a new paradigm through which we can joyfully be His witnesses. Let's complete our homework with our head held high, and our heart looking forward.

I have watched our football team win and lose. It definitely is more fun to win. But sometimes when they are winning, they seem to make a crucial mistake. Instead of playing to keep scoring, they start playing to protect their lead. They started with a strong offense, but then revert to defending their lead. They stop doing what placed them in the lead in the first place. And with this strategy, they often lose the game. In evangelism, the best defense is a good offense!

Today, many people meet Christ at a church. And most church growth in America is through church planting. But something strange happens to many once they reach around 200 people in the church. Suddenly they don't feel as much need to grow. They have plenty of workers to fill the service roles of the church. People start losing their offensive posture, and start relaxing. And then they stop growing.

No, we are not supposed to burn out trying to save the world. Balance is important. But remember, most Christians don't share their faith, and most Christians will never share the plan of salvation with one unbeliever in their entire lifetime... ever! Listen to Paul's invitation:
God has "committed to us the word of reconciliation. Now then, we are ambassadors for Christ, as though God were pleading through us: we implore *you* on Christ's behalf, be reconciled to God" (2 Corinthians 5:19-20).

And here it is in the Message version:
"God has given us the task of telling everyone what he is doing. We're Christ's representatives. God uses us to persuade men and women to drop their differences and enter into God's work of making things right between them. We're speaking for Christ himself now: Become friends with God; he's already a friend with you" (2 Corinthians 5 [19-20])(The Message).

I saw a man playing a clarinet outside the famous Chicago Art Museum. He was an excellent musician. While listening to him, I felt a desire to share my faith with him. When he was finished playing, I approached him and asked, "What is the best thing that has ever happened in your life?" I was so surprised at his answer.

He said Jesus Christ was the best thing in his life! I said, "Do you like to share your faith?" And he responded it absolutely was, and that sharing his faith is his great privilege. In fact, it would be a demotion for him to be the president of the USA, because he's an ambassador for Jesus Christ! (You can see his testimony and hear his incredible playing of his clarinet by going to www.oasisworldministries.org/encounters.)

I was so happy to find a man who was not ashamed of the gospel of Jesus, but wanted to boldly and compassionately declare it whenever and wherever he could.

Let's ask God to rekindle His compassion in our hearts so much that we won't want to keep it in. As I said earlier, when my fears are greater than my compassion, my fears win every time. But, when my compassion is greater than my fears, compassion always wins!

Questions to ponder:
Evangelist Bill Fay says, "God can use your words… He can't use your silence."

What is the greatest hindrance I face that keeps me silent? Am I willing to face it head on?

Action point:
Would you decide right now that you will listen to the Holy Spirit as you read the rest of this book? Ask for His compassion to fill you to overflowing, so it moves you out of your seat and into the street.

11

A CASE FOR PERSONAL EVANGELISM

Verses to remember:
"But you shall receive power when the Holy Spirit has come upon you; and you shall be witnesses to Me" (Acts 1:8)

"These who have turned the world upside down have come here too." (Acts 17:6)

"Therefore he [Paul] reasoned in the synagogue with the Jews and with the *Gentile* worshipers, and in the marketplace daily with those who happened to be there." (Acts 17:17)

I got saved when I was about 12-years-old. I fell head over heels in love with Jesus. He was not just a ticket-out-of-hell. He was my permission to live life to the fullest. He was the "Garden of Eden" blooming the sweet aroma of His presence into my life every day.

The sky looked bluer, my heart felt lighter, and an unusual peace flooded my heart as if I was never to be alone again. I knew I was changed... forever. If that wasn't enough, I was blessed to have a godly home, a wonderful church, and the opportunity to travel on some mission trips that helped ignite my fire even more. Life was good!

I thought all Christians felt this way, but I found that many have lost their joy and peace along the way. They don't have a spring in their step. They look like they are going through the motions of some religious ceremony, trying to connect again, without it costing them too much. They claim to be saved and love God, but they don't seem whole or healed. They can't have fun in a bar, and don't seem to enjoy being in church. What a drag!

I thought the whole world would want this Jesus. But I realized that, while they too were certainly looking for answers to life's hard questions, they definitely were not running to the church to find them. In fact, the church seemed to be irrelevant in their mind... even legalistic and "holier-than-thou." This religious structure did not even show up on most of their radars. And if it did, it seemed to be forgotten by the time Sunday afternoon football had begun.

When I was 19-years-old, I was eager to hang with college-age kids who were also passionate for Jesus. I knew a few, but many seemed to be distracted by their pursuit of education or car payments... or girls. Don't get me wrong, I was in the market for a good-looking girl too, but I was sure I wanted one that was just as passionate about the Lord as I was.

I found a Tuesday night meeting at a discipleship house on Park Avenue in Minneapolis... aptly called *Park House*. A friend invited me and told me it was great. He was right. The place was packed with college-age kids in their jeans, bare feet and long hair. It didn't seem religious in the sense of the old-school approach. But it certainly seemed religious in a good way as they passionately sang their newly written spirit-songs to the Lord. A newly saved, former druggie would then preach from the Bible the same messages I had heard all my life. He was full of fire and energy. Listening to him was like trying to take a drink from a fire hydrant. He just spewed out his love for the Lord unashamedly, and us kids drank in deeply. Then, he would give an opportunity for people to get saved... right there on the spot. And people did.

We ended up starting a church with 50 rag-tag, hippie-type people. It grew from 50 to 2,500 in 12 years. How, you say? In my opinion there were two factors:

> God's sovereign mercy on the hippie generation... and personal evangelism.

That's right, people were simply telling their friends how God had changed their lives. They invited, and often insisted their friends too come with them to church. Some would make a game out of it and see how many of their friends would come and get saved. After experiencing the sweet presence of the Lord in praise and worship, and then hearing the anointed preachers, they were ready to leave their sin behind. And God moved around the world like this in the lives of thousands of college kids. It became known as the Jesus People movement.

This church was unlike any other church in the city. I think we were the first church to actually use a drum set for the glory of God. It wasn't just for the bar scene anymore. God was being praised on the "high sounding cymbals" (Psalm 150, KJV). I think He loved it. I remember the pastor preached about tithes and offerings one Sunday morning. I counted 25 people at the altars giving their lives to Christ at the end of his message. This was happening every week for 12 years. It was normal Christianity.

So where has the church gone wrong? God knows. But I think it has a lot to do with us buying into our culture's thought that religion is a personal thing not to be discussed... sort of like discussing politics at a funeral.

Here's my take. I agree it is personal, but it is certainly not private.

It is the most personal decision a person can ever make... even greater than their choice for marriage. This decision redirects your whole thinking process. It changes how you view life forever.

But private? Jesus wasn't aware it was supposed to be private. He died very publicly. He was very clear that this gospel was for all people of all nations. His mandate was clear... "Go into all the world and preach the gospel to every creature" (Mark 16:15). The disciples sure didn't know it was supposed to be private. They took the message to the whole then-known world. Eleven of the twelve died a martyr's death... publicly. But private faith will rob us and others.

SO WHAT'S IN IT FOR ME?
Most of us listen to our favorite radio station, *WIFM... "What's In It For Me?"* We wonder how this will benefit our lives. Good question! Here are my thoughts.

First, when I share my faith, my fire ignites all over again. I come back to my first love! Getting saved was the best thing in my life, and when I relive it, I get excited!

Second, when I share my faith, I please the heart of God. He was hoping one of the ways I would say "thank you" for saving me is I would tell others about His great love.

Third, when I share my faith, other people's spiritual eyes are opened. They begin to see their own sin, and understand their total need for God's help.

Fourth, when I share my faith, all heaven leans forward and watches. If the person repents of their sin, heaven starts the party! And you get the joy of knowing another person's name is written in the Lamb's Book of Life.

As I am writing this, I am in India on a two day break from our ministry. Just now a 19 year-old man was sweeping the floor at my hotel. I stopped typing to introduce myself and see if I could get a conversation going with him. He spoke broken English, but his English seemed good compared to my very broken Telegu. I introduced myself and told him I was wondering if I could ask him a question. He said yes, so I asked him, "What is the greatest thing that has ever happened to you?" He kept sweeping, and I thought he did not understand. So I repeated the question. He said, "I heard you and I am thinking." After what seemed to be a long pause he replied, "the best thing that happened to me was when a man who lives near me invited me to his church. I heard the praise and worship, and I found out who was the real king... Jesus Christ." I asked, "Did you give your life to Jesus?" He smiled and said, "yes!"

Not only was I talking to a perfect stranger about his faith, but I found out a neighbor had also decided his faith was not private. As a result, this man passed from death to life.

If knowing Jesus is private, then we cannot and should not share Christ with anyone unless they ask us. Their fate is then sealed with eternal doom.

But if knowing Jesus is public, then we can and should share Him with everyone. Their fate is then open to be blessed with eternal life in heaven... and a great peace while on earth.

Personal evangelism is what will turn our world upside-down! It worked for the disciples, and it can work for us.

Questions to ponder:
Will you take it public? _____

When? _____

Action point:
Read stories of martyrs in *Foxe's Book of Martyrs*, or the book *Jesus Freak*. The next time you get together with your friends, bring up one of the more interesting stories. Ask people what they think. Generate discussion on topics that really matter.

12

THE NEED FOR MODERN EVANGELISM

Verse to remember:
"I have become all things to all people so that by all possible means I might save some." ~ Paul
1 Corinthians 9:22 (NIV)

It was going to be scary and fun at the same time. I had the unprecedented opportunity to speak to nearly 8,000 students in five of India's Christian schools. Most of the students were from Hindu homes, but students were sent here because the Christian education was better than public schools. I thought, "I don't know if I can relate. I wish my adult sons were here to take my place. I don't know if I can do this." But I began to ask myself what students liked and how they thought. It wasn't long before I remembered they just like to have fun. So I decided to make the gospel fun. I presented what I call my *Snickers Bar Routine*. It's where I ask for six volunteers to come on stage with me. They are a little nervous, thinking I may embarrass them in front of their friends. Once I have all six on stage, I pull out my bag of Snickers chocolate candy bars. Now the rest of the student body wished they had volunteered! I give the first three people each a candy bar, and then I give the same three another one, and then once more I give the same three students a third candy bar. The whole student body is laughing hysterically, because the last three students got left out.

At the end I give the moral of my skit. I said, "Life isn't always fair. You have a good education, but many children in the world have little or none. Your parents make a good income, but 50% of the world makes $4/day or less. You have good health, but many children suffer all their lives with terrible pain or sicknesses. There is only one thing all people have alike. And that is God loves them and has made a way for them to go to heaven when they die, if they choose it. This gift of God's love is for everyone. Those who know His love must share it with others who don't."

Next I presented the gospel in a clear fashion, explaining the ABCs of following Christ...

> A—ADMIT that I have sinned and done wrong in my life.
> B—BELIEVE that Jesus took my penalty when He died and rose again for me.
> C—CONFESS my sins to Jesus and ask Him to be the One, True God of my life.

Then I asked them to bow their heads and pray with me if they would like to be forgiven by Jesus. Conservatively, at least 6,000 of the 8,000 students raised their hands and prayed a stirring and heart-felt prayer of repentance. Wow!

What does Paul mean... "I have become all things to all people so that by all possible means I might save some" (1 Corinthians 9:22) (NIV)? Paul surely never condoned compromising his faith or becoming ashamed of it. He simply tried to get into their heads and understand what they were looking for in life. He realized everyone is at a different spiritual stage of development in their quest for truth. But everyone... is... searching.

I must embrace the old adage "Same message... different methods." Sometimes we think we have to make a major change in our approach, but it is not always true. A professional baseball coach may advise his batter to change a little thing like stepping forward more in the batter's box, or gripping his bat a little higher. The game doesn't change, just how you approach it.
The late Bill Bright, founder of Campus Crusade for Christ, the most effective evangelistic ministry in modern times, said something like this, "I think 50% of Americans would turn their lives to Christ if the gospel was lovingly presented to them by someone they trusted."

Barna research company found even better statistics... 75% of Americans are willing to listen to someone they trust share about their spiritual journey.

So, how do we build trust? Do you like it when a salesperson gets pushy? I sure don't, and I think we are all the same. We get defensive. So if I get aggressive in sharing the gospel, I can easily put them on the defensive. We have to find a way to reach people that won't cause them to put their defensive shield up. We have to treat people with respect.

I have two pet peeves. One is when other cars follow me very closely. The other is, you may have guessed it, pushy salespeople. One day I had just finished my devotions, and I was feeling real spiritual. I was looking through the want ads for a used car, and found one that I wanted to learn more about. I certainly wasn't ready to buy, but I needed to start learning about this car model, so I called a car dealer and talked to a salesman named Johnny. He was very pleasant over the phone, but soon began asking pointed questions like, "are you going to come in and look at the car?" And, "What time will you be here?" And, "What's your blood type?" (not really). I replied, "You're sort of pushy, aren't you!?" He said he needed to make a living for his family. I sensed myself losing patience fast, and finally ended the call abruptly by saying in a terse tone, "If I come, I come. If I don't, I don't. Goodbye." I felt guilty losing my patience so quickly, especially since I had just finished a wonderful time in prayer and the word. But this guy hit my hot button. And I didn't like it that I could be controlled by him. But something was different. God was talking to me the whole time I was talking to Johnny. Do you know what God spoke to my heart? "This man needs the Lord."

Now I was trapped. I had asked God that morning to use me for His glory. But, I had already lost patience with Johnny on the phone, and didn't really want to humble myself and call him back. So God let me think about it.

It seems that being *modern* in my approach to reaching people for Christ requires me to be *old-fashioned* in my manner and attitude. In other words, God was requiring me to be humble and to lay down my rights if I wanted to reach this guy. I had a choice. Either humble myself and love Johnny where he was at, or lose the opportunity, in which case God would surely find someone else to reach Johnny.

But I had a good problem... *holy stubbornness.* I didn't want God to find someone else... I wanted Him to use me! And by God's grace, I chose to listen and act!

It was sort of like Queen Esther when she was told by her uncle Mordecai that maybe God put her in this position "for *such* a time as this" (Esther 4:14). And that if she didn't step up to save her Jewish people, God would find someone else. At our core, I think we really want God to use us. We don't want Him to find someone else.

So I swallowed hard, and hit the redial button on the phone. I wasn't sure what I was going to say. I just knew I wanted to "adapt" so God could trust me again with another assignment. That's the word I am looking for... "adapt." We are real good at asking others to adapt to our thinking, but not so good at being tolerant of others. We want the fish to be cleaned before we catch them. Please read this next passage slowly.

> God loves sinners as they are. He draws them with His lovingkindness. He cleans them up later.

I called Johnny and told him I was coming in to see him. As I walked into the car showroom and asked for Johnny, I was nervous knowing I needed to apologize. It's hard to witness to someone when you've hung up on him. After greeting him, I said, "I am the one who lost patience with you on the phone. I am sorry... I just don't like to be pressured." I guess it was a half-apology... sort of.

We got into the car and took it for a drive on the freeway. He was talking about the great benefits of the car. After a few miles we pulled up to a stoplight, and he looked at me and said the weirdest thing... "you have a glow around you."

I thought he had been watching too many *Star Trek* movies. We pulled back into the used car parking lot. I said, "Johnny, that glow that you sensed is the Spirit of the Lord Jesus." And I began to explain to him the whole plan of salvation. He was listening to every word. When I was done, I said, "What would hinder you from surrendering your life to Jesus today?" He said, "Nothing." I thought this was way too simple. So I explained the plan of salvation again. And again the third time. Finally I realized this man wanted to get right with God. And so, while sitting in the car, he prayed with me to make Jesus his Lord. And heaven listened and rejoiced!

And what was just as exciting was this... I had really heard God! And I had obeyed. I hadn't blown it or messed it up. I came close, but God showed me how to overlook his sales methods, and love the person instead. Modern evangelism must be flexible... and be willing to adapt to each situation, each person, each need. That's how God loved us. He met us where we were. He didn't make us come to Him... He came to us! Hallelujah.

13

THE URGENCY FOR MISSIONAL EVANGELISM

I read about a university class reunion where graduates from 40 years earlier had gathered. During the course of the reunion a survey was taken. On the survey they asked every graduate from 40 years earlier if they had written down goals for their life while they were in college. Surprisingly, only 3% of the graduates had done so. Even more surprising was the fact that these 3% had accumulated more wealth than the other 97% combined! Intentional? Yes. Strategic? Yes.

> "Write the vision
> And make *it* plain on tablets,
> That he may run who reads it."
> (Habakkuk 2:2)

Pastor Thimothi Rao is the director of our ministry in India. He has intentionally and strategically posted a list of his church's yearly goals prominently on a wall of his church. This way everybody can see it and pray over it. This is a great way to share vision. However, there is another list he could post if he listened to his fears. This is a list of strong motivators which are familiar to all of us. Fear of failure, rejection, and what people might think are common phobias. We either run from them… or at them.

Of what are we afraid? Failure? Yes, but mostly I think we are afraid of ourselves. We have developed a list that is just the opposite of a *goal list*. Our *fear list* ranks the things of which we are more concerned about than success. After all, success always involves risk.

Of some things I am no longer afraid. Falling off my bicycle is no longer an issue. When I was 5-years-old, it was. Passing my driver's test, raising children and preaching a sermon are no longer things of which I am fearful. At one time, they were all a great concern. But I had training, had a few falls in life which proved not to be fatal, and decided that some things should come off my *fear list* and be placed on my *goal list*. Removing "raising children" from my list was a gradual process. But within a few months of having our first child, I could safely say that I had learned a lot about life and love from becoming a parent. Vicki and I soon started thinking strategically about when to have our second child, and prayerfully considering how many children God wanted us to bear.

But there are times when the fear of failure is stronger than the anticipated joy of success. The great baseball hero Babe Ruth said, "Every strike brings me closer to the next home run." Failure is simply another opportunity to succeed!

It's the same way with sharing our faith. Good intentions are often interrupted by our fears. As many times as I have shared my faith, often I still fight fear. Evangelist Billy Graham said every time he got into the pulpit at his crusades, he had butterflies in his stomach. Fear seems to be a universal language. It is a warning system that alerts us to new territory and uncomfortable circumstances. This is where we must be both intentional and strategic!

INTENTIONAL EVANGELISM

For years when writing letters, I have often concluded with the personalized ending: "Intentional for souls, Tom Elie." What does this mean? It means my *intent* is clearly defined. My goal has a deadline. As far as I am concerned, my desire will one day become a reality. My hope will be fulfilled. Don't we want to see our God-given dreams come to pass? Don't we want to practice what we preach? Yes we do! There is something within every one of us that wants what's real, and not fantasy. We want reality, not just theory. How does this happen?

Do you remember the story Jesus told of two brothers who were asked to accomplish a task? (Matthew 21:28) The first brother said "I will not" but later went and did it. The second brother said "I will..." (NIV) but didn't do it. I know I have been the second brother plenty of times in my life. But down deep we want to obey our Master, the Lord Jesus Christ. We want to hear His voice, and then actually do what He says.

No fisherman ever learned to fish without putting a line in the water. He then probably endured watching his bobber and line for hours at a time without a nibble. He was learning, but only because he put the line in the water. One pastor said, "we used to never pray for the sick, and we never saw people healed. Now we pray regularly for the sick, and we regularly see some healed!" If we want to see people come to Christ, we have to engage pre-believers in conversation, and find ways to care for them at their point of need. We... are... fishers... of... men. I didn't say it... Jesus did (Mark 1:17). We must get a line in the water. Let's go fishing and see what happens!

It also takes us being honest with ourselves. Repeat with me... "I am not superman, and I am not bullet-proof." There, wasn't that freeing? We must admit our weaknesses, our failures, and our inconsistencies. We must admit we are tired of depending on ourselves for our next surge of strength. Let's get rid of the guilt of evangelism by telling the Lord we can't do it on our own. We realize it truly is "'Not by might nor by power, but by My Spirit,' says the LORD..." (Zechariah 4:6).

Do you know how freeing this is to admit our total dependence on God? My only job is to do whatever He says (John 2:5). Intentionality says "Let's do it." Let's not just talk about it. It's getting off the church pew and taking the first step as God directs you. It means no more excuses... no more rationalizing.... no more delays. It's means keeping the main thing the main thing.

Intentional witnessing means I will pray every day God will use me today for His glory as He directs. It means I am available today. It means my tongue belongs to God... my feet belong to God. Why do you think the word says "How beautiful are the feet of those who bring good news!" (Romans 10:15 [See also Isaiah 52:7]) (NIV)? Why do you think the word says "Wear shoes that are able to speed you on as you preach the Good News of peace with God." (Ephesians 6:15) (TLB)? Feet in action are intentionally walking somewhere. Some people are just walking in circles. But many others are taking steps to get out of the boat, and intentionally walk where they have never walked before. Feet are meant for walking!

I think Jesus was a rapper. He said in Matthew 28:20, "lo, I am with you always." That's King James modern-speak for "yo." He says "If you'll go, 'yo,' I'll go with you." We're never alone... "Yo"... get your feet movin' boy!

So... let's walk! Let's do the works of Jesus purposefully, and not accidentally. Let's do the works of Jesus with grace and not legalism. Let's do the works of Jesus with urgency and not apathy. Let's serve others out of love! Will you take that step?

Good intentions alone won't finish the task. Someone said, "The road to hell is paved with good intentions." But I believe the road to heaven is paved with good strategy. Read on.

STRATEGIC EVANGELISM
"A goal without a deadline is just a dream."
To be strategic is the second step after being intentional. The apostle Peter has given preachers many great practical illustrations with his life. He was known for both his decisiveness and his cowardice. He was known for both his faith and his fears. He was real... just like you and me. Let's learn from him.

Peter and the disciples are in the midst of a huge storm, and they think their boat is about to sink. About three a.m., after nine hours of rowing and getting nowhere, Jesus comes walking on the water towards them. He knows He will scare them, but more than that, He wants them to learn a lesson. He desires that they would not solve their problems in the natural, but instead turn to the supernatural. In other words, you can row all night in your own strength and get nowhere, or you can turn to the power of the Spirit within you and see supernatural results. Once they realize He is not a ghost, Peter has a brilliant idea. "Lord, if it is You, command me to come to You on the water" (Matthew 14:28). And Jesus takes him up on his idea. "Come" was the only invitation Peter needed to hear. In fact without that one word, he surely would have sunk. But with that invitation, Peter lifted his left leg over the edge of the boat, intentionally.

I must not only take a step out of the boat like Peter did, but as I begin to walk on water, I must have a plan for two things. One, how to keep from sinking. Two, how to arrive at my destination successfully.

So how do I keep from sinking? Keep your eyes on Jesus.

As long as Peter kept his eyes on Jesus, he supernaturally walked on water. Only when his eyes shifted to the waves swirling around his feet did his fears creep in. The voice of fear is resident within us all the time. We decide if we are going to listen to it or not. When driving a car in the USA, I have no fear. When riding in a car in India, my fears rise to the surface quickly. What brings confidence in one situation can bring fear if the circumstances change. So the real question is, "How can I starve my fears, and feed my faith?"

One sunny afternoon I was walking along the shores of the Bay of Bengal in India, and I came upon some fishing boats. Inside, the men were sleeping, and one woke up as I peeked inside. His eyes were bloodshot and red. He told me that all the fishermen begin their day around four p.m., and then fish all night. Do you remember Peter and his pals were out fishing all night and caught nothing? Sometimes our strategies need adjustment. What is a good strategy for one day might not be the best for the next day. This is where being led by the Spirit comes in. Did Jesus have an idea for Peter? Yes, He said, "Cast the net on the right side of the boat, and you will find *some*" (John 21:6). Peter and his pals had just finished washing their nets and putting them away. This was a lot of work to take them out again, and launch their boats, only to put the nets on the other side. It must have seemed silly, yet Peter knew the voice of Jesus. Better yet, he *trusted* the voice of Jesus.

I starve my fears by training myself to know and cherish His voice. He speaks as I slowly read and ponder His words, and as I daily quiet myself in my secret place. Our whole life is a journey in both getting to know and learning to trust our Savior's voice. Sometimes our strategies work well, and sometimes they seem to bring less fruit. Our job is to obey His voice, and He will bring the fruit... some 30, some 60 and some 100-fold.

Please listen close. This is one of the most important things I believe God has ever taught me. Here goes... are you ready? My time with God is the foundation for my work for God. Please read it again. "My time *with* God is the foundation for my work *for* God." It's all about relationship!

I cannot give fresh water to others if I am not drinking deeply myself. This is where we get our role in life messed up. We are so busy doing God's work, we don't have time to be with Him. We think God needs us! No... We need relationship with God!

In Mark 28 Jesus is getting ready to leave the earth. He is giving His **final instructions** to His disciples. This is a pretty heavy moment. If I am a disciple, I don't want to miss His final words. He sent them to the mountain to which He had appointed them. Jesus was accustomed to going to his prayer mountain... alone.... to meet with God. Now He is also appointing them to their own prayer mountain. It's in prayer and the word that we hear God's voice. I need my alone time with God to hear what His Spirit says to me.

~ Our first priority in life is to develop relationship with
God through prayer and meditating on the word.

~ Our second priority in life is to develop relationship to our family.

~ Our third priority in life is to develop relationship to others.

This strategy alone will launch you into a wondrous new world of both rest for your weary soul, and new excitement for your journey ahead!

PEANUT BUTTER AND JELLY GOSPEL

In Matthew 28 Jesus gives His final words to His disciples. He gives them a command to be both intentional and strategic. Here it is: "Go... and make disciples."

These two commands go together, like peanut butter and jelly! "Go" is the operative word. Unless I go, I cannot "make disciples." This is the problem in the church today. When we stop *going*, we are cleaning the same fish... over and over. It's time to catch *new* fish. I've heard many pastors and leaders say, "I'm called more to discipleship," implying that someone else should do the evangelism. Yet, many people in their own churches are not being discipled. I've heard many say we should not evangelize if we are not going to disciple, implying they are not called to evangelize... only to disciple. This would be like a married couple saying, "We are not called to bear children, only to raise them."

Let's talk about "Go." Please listen to the heart of Jesus. He Himself defined His mission very precisely. He had no doubts as to His earthly assignment.

> "For the Son of Man has come to seek and to save that which was lost" (Luke 19:10).

Evangelism *is* part of discipleship. If we separate the two, we will stop giving birth. In fact, "Go" is 2/3rds of God's name! Discipleship must include teaching others to share their faith. If every Christian saw two people come to Christ, and then discipled so they also shared their faith with two people per year, the whole world could be reached in a very short time!

Historically, most new moves of God that form into a denomination do not keep their pure tenets of faith for more than two generations. Likewise, most church growth in the USA today comes from new church plants. It's only when we want to grow through *new* spiritual births that we move the gospel ahead. Christianity has been in a severe decline in Europe for years. I am told that many of the historical church buildings are now being used as Muslim mosques. Through new births alone, France's population will soon have a Muslim majority. Muslim families continue to value childbirth, while most Europeans diminish it.
Likewise, when the church values training of existing believers without an emphasis on evangelism, we cannot grow. A person is not a mature Christian unless they embrace evangelism as part of their privilege and duty before the Lord.

Wait a minute... back up the car. Duty? I haven't heard that word recently unless it's associated with the Army. We don't like duty. It makes us feel trapped, controlled and obligated. We want to be free to express ourselves any way we desire. But let's think this through. Do you always *feel* like cleaning the house, washing the car or walking the dog on a freezing morning? I didn't always *feel* like studying for my school tests, or going to work on Monday morning, or tithing or doing bills, or... the list could go on and on.

Duty can be our friend. I don't always *feel* like sharing my faith, do you? But what if we all lived by how we *feel* spiritually? People wouldn't share their faith, pastors wouldn't prepare for their sermons and we would only pray and read the Bible when we *felt* led. You get the drift... our feelings are not supposed to lead our lives. Holy desire increases when we purposely draw close to God, regardless of how we feel. "Draw near to God and He will draw near to you" (James 4:8). In fact, the best time to draw close to God is when you don't feel like it. Paul and Silas praised the Lord in prison at midnight, the darkest hour. They had just been beaten and now they were tied tightly in a prison stockade. Praising was the last thing they *felt* like doing.

But they did it anyhow. Why? They knew the power of God went deeper than their momentary feelings. They had previously decided to praise God at all times. So they acted on their *previous* decision when times got tough. They were not fair-weather believers. They were in this for the long haul... through thick and thin. They didn't pick and choose what they wanted from their relationship with God. They knew serving God would cost them everything.
Listen to Jesus' words in Luke 17:10. He tells of some servants who came home from a long and tiring day of work in the fields, only to first make dinner for their Master before they rested. They didn't complain about their hard day. They were just glad to have a job. "So likewise [in similar fashion] you, when you have done all those things which you are commanded, say, 'We are unprofitable servants. We have done what was our duty to do'" (Luke 17:10). Evangelism is both our privilege and duty. After all, we are debtors.

If you were unsaved and heading to hell, would you want others to be compassionately bold enough to share Christ's love with you? Isn't this part of what Jesus meant when He said to "love your neighbor as yourself" (Mark 12:31)?

Some people say this is not my calling. We may have different gifts and different callings. Some are called to the office of a teacher. But Jesus was the greatest teacher ever! He was the greatest pastor (the good shepherd), the greatest apostle and the greatest prophet... but He was also the greatest evangelist. Evangelism is part of discipleship. One who thinks they are a mature Christian must also allow their heart to be broken for the lost, and then obey what God puts in their heart. We must be finished with lame and weak excuses.

If we don't "Go," then who will reach the pre-believers? I will tell you who will influence them.
The Jehovah's Witnesses will.
The Mormons will.
The Hindus and Muslims will.
Nominal and lukewarm Christianity will begin to stifle us.

You see the urgency, don't you? So why are we still on earth? To influence as many people as possible for Jesus. Everyone around us has a spiritual void. We are all looking for purpose and meaning in life. And we have their answer! "Go" is for every believer. It is our mandate from God. And it is our holy duty and privilege.

But the second part is how to arrive at my destination successfully. We must have a strategy to see the fruit last. Once we start going, we must win them to Christ and disciple those who are willing to be discipled. How will we win them, and how will we disciple them? This is one of Christianity's greatest questions. I think the answer is less complicated than we think. Get ready for a surprise.

(Hint: When I first disciple myself to share my faith, I can then disciple others to do the same. Only then do we stop "cleaning the same fish." Only then do we have new people to disciple. Only then can the church be a healthy model of the older discipling the younger.)

When will you become intentional? Today, next week or next year? Someone once said, "Nothing happens without a deadline."

Question to ponder:
Do you know how freeing it is to admit your total dependence upon God?

Action point:
Apply Habakkuk 2:2 right now, and write down what you would like God to do through your witness for Him, and when you will start.

_____

_____

_____

_____

14

THE *ONE MINUTE WITNESS* TRAINING TOOL

Here is my book's only disclaimer.

This evangelism tool is simply an aid to help you share the life-changing story of Jesus. We must remember it is only a tool... nothing more... nothing less. It is not the message... it is only the messenger. We must put our confidence in the leading of the Holy Spirit, and His ability to draw all men unto Himself. There is no magic tool that works every time, or that should even be followed to the letter every time. We are to be led of the Holy Spirit. The tool is my helper with a small letter "h." The Holy Spirit is my helper with a capital letter "H."

And if we want to help make fruit-bearing disciples, our strategy should be to disciple ourselves first to be effective in evangelism. When should I share my faith? How do I know to whom I should talk?

The best time to initiate a time of evangelism is at the leading of the Holy Spirit. Jesus often approached strangers... the woman at the well, Zacheaus who was up in the tree, Nicodemus who came at night to Jesus, and Matthew the tax collector when Jesus said, "Follow Me". Other times He shared after building relationships. But He only did what the Father told Him.

I dare you to pray this prayer daily: *"Dear Lord Jesus, I am available today to be Your voice. Please open my heart and my eyes to someone in need. Amen."*

One day I was seated next to a man in an airplane. I didn't *feel* like sharing my faith. In fact, 50% of the time I don't feel led. That's because my flesh doesn't always desire the will of God. As I was sitting there, I remembered what my good friend, Darrell Dobbelmann told me one day. Darrell has been used by God in a missions organization called Dove International to take American Christians on short-term, third world missions trips. He has led more than 200 group trips. He told me he prays this kind of prayer often... "Lord, I am available today." So I prayed that prayer on the airplane. Before I knew it, this man was initiating conversation. Before you knew it, I was showing him pictures of our last India trip. And he said he wanted to come with me to India on one of our trips. Who knows what is behind each opportunity? Let's just be available... everyday.

I have used this *ONE MINUTE WITNESS* tool in different cultures, different countries, and with people very different from myself. I have also used it many times with people that seem to be like myself. I can say without fail, people have listened intently when I approach them respectfully. Why? The Holy Spirit is already at work in everyone, drawing them to the truth of Jesus. Your testimony helps confirm this truth in their hearts.

This tool will be a win-win for you. You are simply sharing your story. It's not about selling or convincing. It's not about any political party. It's not Catholic, Jewish or Protestant. It's not asking people to come to your church, or discussing church doctrine. It is simply the story of what has personally happened to you! And people love stories!

Are you ready to start learning this faith-sharing tool? But here's a warning: it could change the way you do life forever!

ONE MINUTE WITNESS

www.oneminutewitness.org
(You can see the entire tool online plus the video teaching of the tool. You can use it in your small group to train, practice and go do it!)

1. PERMISSION

Here's a bit of trivia. Years ago the storybook character Mary Poppins sang a famous Disney song that said... "just a spoonful of _____ helps the medicine go down."

Here is the question that has stumped me and every other soul-searching Christian I know: How do I transition my conversations with people so I can talk about Jesus? How do I turn the topic towards Christ casually, without preaching at them?

Here is the best medicine and best answer I've found: PERMISSION.

When we ask permission to share something, people enjoy saying "yes." Their defenses come down when we treat them with respect.

People don't feel like you are trying to force something down their throat. The old Disney song said it well... "Just a spoonful of *sugar* helps the medicine go down." It's true. Permission is the sugar. When we ask permission, people feel like they are 'in control'. Permission brings a smile to people's faces.

Here's how I start or transition my conversation...

"I was wondering, is it okay if I ask you a question?" Unless they are busy doing something else, they always agree. People feel respected. Permission granted.
After they agree, I pop the question...
"What would you say is the best thing that has ever happened to you?"

People invariably smile, and repeat the question back to me. They love the question. Why? Because it forces them to dig into their memory archives and bring up a pleasant thought. I can almost guarantee you that no one has *ever* asked them this question. Yet it is intriguing to everyone.

What's their response? Many people say getting married or having their children was their high point in life. Some say finishing their schooling, or landing a job of their dreams was the best thing. Some sadly say nothing great has happened to them yet. I had one man say his greatest moment was catching a 36 inch walleye fish. He even invited me to his truck to see the photo! It was huge, and he was proud. (Obviously he was not married yet. If he was, he would not have wanted to give that answer if his wife was listening!)

What's my response? Listen and enjoy.

Listen not only to what they are saying, but to what they are not saying. Do they find their fulfillment in relationships, accomplishments or in possessions? Try to remember what they said, for you may be able to include it later in your conversation, especially if you can link it to your own story. For example: "I know what you mean. I thought I could find my greatest joy in relationships. But then I found that it didn't quite satisfy the way I had hoped it would."

Enjoy their moment of joy as they describe this highlight. Don't just listen so you can get to your part. But listen and enjoy it as a fellow human being that knows we need some good memories now and then to perk us up. As my friend Bruce Schoeman says, "They should not be viewed as targets, but as friends." The Bible also instructs us to "Rejoice with those who rejoice" (Romans 12:15). When they are done, one of two things can happen. Often, they will then ask you, "Well, how about you? What's the best thing that ever happened to you?"

Or, when the two of you are finished talking about their greatest moment, you can ask them this question...

"May I share the greatest thing that has ever happened to me?"

Because you have shown interest in their life, they will now be willing to listen to your story... if it is brief. We want our whole story to be condensed to approximately 60 seconds. We live in a "sound byte" era where people want the facts, and not necessarily all the details. In other words, don't run up every rabbit trail with stories of how you loved grandma's oatmeal cookies, etc. Keep it brief and to the point. You will keep your audience listening.

And so we start our story...

2. B.C. (Before Christ)

We all have a "B.C." That's right, 'BEFORE CHRIST.' What was your life like before you personally fell in love with Christ?

I didn't say before you went to church... before you were confirmed or baptized... or before you got religious. I mean when you truly became 'born again', or a whole-hearted follower of Jesus Christ.

Try to recall what your life looked like before you surrendered to Christ. Recreate your time of personal searching. Here's how my testimony starts...

> "Well, I have been blessed with a wonderful wife and family. But that's not the best thing. There was a time in my life when..."

Here's where you start writing your story.

First, I want you to think of three adjectives to describe your B.C. life. Maybe you felt loneliness, frustration, success without significance, no peace, or a lack of purpose. Maybe you felt guilty, angry at life or God, or just ho-hum about life.

Maybe things were going pretty good, but you were frustrated that you didn't know what would happen to you after you die.

Finish this sentence with those three adjectives or phrases... "There was a time in my life when..."

My testimony goes something like this:

> "I have a wonderful wife and family. But that's not the best thing. Years ago, there was a time in my life when

I was looking for my purpose, wondering what happens when I die, and feeling guilty over some things I had done wrong."

You can insert your own words to describe what you remember. By the way, invariably when I finish that sentence, people start nodding their heads in agreement. I can be talking to a perfect stranger, and instantly they are relating to what I am saying, and admitting it!

Now, I know what some of you are thinking. "I can't remember last month, much less what I felt like so long ago." Or "I grew up in a Christian home, and I don't remember an exact time when I gave my life to Christ."

Here's my experience. I grew up in a Christian home. I came to Christ when I was around 12-years-old. I don't remember a specific time of asking Jesus into my life. But I can safely assume a few things:

~ First, like most people, I was wondering what my purpose was on earth.

~ Second, because I had sinned, I had no peace in my heart.

~ Third, I was wondering where I was going when I died.

So, as I revisit these things, my story begins to take shape. Go ahead, pause a moment and think what your life was like B.C.

What three adjectives or phrases describe your B.C. life? Go ahead and fill in the blanks below. Take a few minutes right here to remember what your life was like. If you draw a blank, work backwards as to the reasons you currently know you need Christ.

"There was a time in my life when..."

1. _____

2. _____

3. _____

3. T.P. (Turning Point)

Everyone has a time in the past where they started to see their own spiritual need. I think most people have one, but have forgotten about it. It's the time when your spiritual curiosity kicked in. It's when your conscience began to bother you. It's when you started hearing God talk to you, but weren't sure what or who it was. This was your turning point. Let's try to remember it right now. Maybe someone invited you to a church service where you sensed the presence of God for the first time in a long time. Or perhaps you faced a crisis in your life that forced you to call out to God. Maybe you lost a loved one, and you started thinking about where you would spend eternity. Or you found great success, only to find it didn't fill your void as you thought it would.

What happened in your life that started you on your own personal, spiritual quest? This is a very important part of your story. Everybody will relate with you because they have all had times when they desperately cried out to God for help.

For me, I don't remember an actual event that triggered my searching. But I do know that when I went to church and heard about a God who loves me personally, I desperately wanted to know this God. This was certainly a time of transformation for me. So for me, my Turning Point sounds like this:

"But one day someone told me about a God who really loves me...and even likes me. In fact He wants me to live in Heaven with Him forever. But I found I was not eligible, because heaven's perfect, and I'm certainly not. But God made a way for me to get there by sending His son Jesus to die for me and my sin. Then He rose from the dead to prove He was really God. So I asked Jesus to forgive me and become the leader of my life instead of me."

What's your Turning Point? Write it down:

_____

_____

_____

_____

4. A.D. (Anno Domini- After Christ)

What's today's date? At the end of today's calendar date is our current year, followed by "A.D." I used to think A.D. meant "after death." But it doesn't. It really means "Anno Domini" ... two Latin words that mean "the year of our Lord." In fact, our whole earth's calendar system is based on the life and death of Jesus Christ!

This is perhaps the easiest and most fun part of our testimony. We want to find three adjectives to describe the positive change that Christ has made in our lives. That's not too hard, is it?

Having new joy, a sense of purpose, fulfillment, assurance of going to heaven when I die, no guilt or new friends are common responses. Experiencing trust, peace and forgiveness are also powerful. The benefits of serving and knowing Christ are endless! It's a picture of the prodigal son coming home in Luke 15, and the father rejoices by saying, "My son was dead and is alive again; he was lost and is found."

My A.D. sounds like this:

> "And now since making Jesus the leader of my life, I have new purpose, real joy and the peace that I know I will go to heaven when I die."

What would you say are the three greatest things you treasure about knowing and serving Jesus? Go ahead and write these benefits down:

1. _____

2. _____

3. _____

5. "IF I HAD NEVER MET CHRIST, I..."

Here is the closer. I want you to imagine what your life would look like today if you never found Jesus as your personal Savior. That's scary, isn't it? I know we don't really know, and probably wouldn't want to know, but go ahead and imagine what it might look like. You certainly would not be reading this book, having daily times with God in prayer and the word, or have the new found blessings you described in A.D.

Some people have said they would be in jail, or on drugs, or divorced or even dead. Some say their whole life would be radically different, all for the worse. Some say they would still be searching and unsatisfied. When you close your testimony with this phrase, the listener has a chance to hear your heart.

My testimony sounds like this at this point:

> "And I know if I had not surrendered my life to Jesus, I might be successful in some areas of life, but I would still be searching for my purpose, like so many people are today."

When I am done, I thank them for listening to me... and I'm done. They are happy I briefly shared from my heart. And I am happy I got to share Jesus with people I really care about. And here's something surprising. Often when I am done, they thank me for sharing with them.

If they are open to talk more, you will know by watching their facial expressions, or respond to their questions. Don't argue church doctrine or about the Bible. The power of your testimony is that it is simply your story.
It's like the blind man that said, "I don't know much about this man who healed me. All I know is I once was blind, but now I see" (paraphrasing John 9:25).

Go ahead... finish this sentence: "If I had never met Christ, I...

_____

_____

_____

_____

LET'S PRACTICE!

Let's suppose you have been praying for your neighbor. You are genuinely concerned about their welfare, and looking now for an opportunity to share your faith. Sharing with a neighbor is definitely different than sharing with a stranger. You have to live near them for quite some time. Hopefully, you will first build relationship with them through acts of kindness and caring. Before you witness to your neighbors, show them you care about them as people, not just targets for your soul-winning goal. Have them over for a BBQ pot luck, or go to a ball game, or attend one of their kid's functions with them. As someone once said, "People don't care how much you know until they know how much you care." Once you have a good relationship, watch and pray for a time when you can share your story. It's really quite simple. Prayer…. Care…. Share!

Here's how my *ONE MINUTE WITNESS* story would usually sound. Remember, you can memorize the tool, but let it come from your heart. It won't always sound the same. I will indicate the five numbers for our *ONE MINUTE WITNESS* tool as we go along so you can identify where it changes. (Are you timing me?)

> Tom: "Hi neighbor, how's your day going?"

> Joe Neighbor: "I guess it's OK. My wife's out of town, so I have some extra responsibility for a few days. Say, how about our football team... do you think there's any hope for them this year?
> (chit-chat about the sport scene, news or weather, etc. Stay non-political.)

> Tom: (1-Permission) "Hey Joe, I like to ask someone a question everyday. Do you mind if I ask you my question?

Joe: "Yea, go ahead."

Tom: "What's the best thing that has ever happened to you in your life?"

Joe: "Wow, that's a good question. I suppose my wife and kids. You know how special they are to me."

Tom: Yes, you sure do have a great family. And we really enjoy having your kids around. It's so fun to watch them grow up. Hey, do you mind if I share the best thing in my life?

Joe: Well, of course... go ahead.

Tom: "Thanks Joe. It seems we have been neighbors for quite a while now, and we've talked about a lot of ordinary stuff in our lives and some serious stuff too. But it occurs to me I've never shared the greatest thing that has ever happened in my life.

(2-BC) As you know, I too have a wonderful wife and family. But that's not the best thing, Joe. Years ago, there was a time in my life when I was looking for my purpose, feeling guilty over some things I had done wrong, and wondering what happens when I die. (3-TP) But somebody told me about a God who loves me, and even likes me. In fact, He wanted me to be in Heaven forever, but I found I was not eligible, because Heaven is perfect and I'm far from it. But this God made a way for me by sending His son Jesus to die for my wrong. Then he rose again to prove He was God. (4-AD) So I asked Jesus, to forgive me and

135

be the new leader of my life. And Joe, it was the best choice I ever made. Now I have new peace, purpose, and a confidence that I will go to heaven when I die. (5-If I had never met Christ...) And I know if I had never given my life to Christ, I would probably be a very arrogant man, still searching for hope and for my purpose. So thanks for listening, and just know He loves you very much too, Joe. And thanks for being a great neighbor!"

Joe: "Well, thanks for sharing with me. I appreciate it."

Chances are, this is the very first time Joe has had a friend share the gospel with him in a respectful manner. Now Joe has the seed of Christ's love clearly planted in his heart by someone he trusts. You can take it further if you feel he is interested. If not, respect where he is and let him process it. Maybe after a couple weeks, you may see him again and casually ask him what he thought about your story, or if he had ever heard a story like that before. God will lead you. Often we sow, and someone else reaps later on. Or sometimes we reap where someone else sowed. Either way, we are partners together, and someday when we get to heaven we will share the fruit of our labors!

You can not only share the *ONE MINUTE WITNESS* with your neighbors, but with a friend at work, the lady at the dry-cleaning counter, the delivery truck driver, someone sitting in the park or... anyone!

So let's review our *ONE MINUTE WITNESS* tool:

1. PERMISSION
2. B.C. (Before Christ)
3. T.P. (Turning Point)
4. A.D. (Anno Domini)
5. IF I HAD NEVER MET CHRIST...

Can you repeat these five points now by memory three times in a row... without looking?

Good. Now try speaking your whole five point testimony out loud right now. Try it out on someone in your family. The more you practice, the better you will get at it. Try to keep it around 60 seconds long... 90 seconds at the most. This will definitely help keep your friend stay interested and engaged in your life story.

Remember, *practice makes perfect!*

Again, you can find the whole *ONE MINUTE WITNESS* tool and video training at:

<u>www.oneminutewitness. org</u>

1.   **Permission** ~ "May I ask you a question?"

     What is the best thing that has ever happened to you?

     May I share the best thing that's ever happened to me?

2.   **B.C.** ~ Describe your life Before Christ.

     "There was a time in my life when…"

     Write three adjectives or phrases.

     1. _____

     2. _____

     3. _____

1. Permission

2. B.C. (Before Christ)

3. T.P. (Turning Point)

4. A.D. (Anno Domini)

5. "If I had not met Christ..."

3.   T.P. ~ What was your Turning Point?
      1. How did you hear about Jesus?

      _____

      2. What did you ask Jesus to do in your life?

      _____

4.   A.D. ~ "Since I met Christ…"
      Describe the positive change Christ has made in your life.
      1. _____
      2. _____
      3. _____

5.   "If I had never met Christ…"
      What would your life look like without Christ?

      _____

15

SAVED!

Have you ever said "no" to God?

I had just finished teaching our *ONE MINUTE WITNESS* faith-sharing seminar on a Sunday night. It was late, but if I left right away, I could drive for three hours and be in my own bed by 1 a.m. (It's strangely exciting anytime you can be in your own bed instead of a hotel bed.)

So I quickly said my good-byes at the church and left town. But I was hungry, so I stopped at a fast-food restaurant. I ordered a hamburger and an ice cream malt. This was going to taste *sooooo* good!

But while I was waiting for my food, the Lord impressed me to share my faith with the lone employee working there. I told God I didn't have time, because I had a long drive home, and I was already tired. Did He want me to risk falling asleep while driving? I paid for my food and quickly ran it out to my car. I set it on the driver's seat while I went to the back seat to get some comfortable clothes to change into. I ran back into the restaurant's restroom to change my clothes, and quickly ran back to the car. I jumped into the driver's seat, eager to start my long drive home.

But something was wrong. I forgot my ice cream malt was also in the driver's seat. I realized I had sat on it, and now ice cream was all over my car seat, my clothes and everywhere! I felt so dumb. How could I do this? I had to run back into the restaurant, get some wet towels, and quickly clean up this terrible mess!

And while I was cleaning my car, the Lord started talking to me. He said, "Tom, what are you doing?" I told Him I had to clean this up or it would start smelling badly. He said, "so you have time to clean up your mess, but no time to share your faith with the man in the restaurant?" I was humbled.

So I returned to the restaurant, and told the man about my accident. He was sympathetic, and made me another malt for free. And then I did what I was supposed to do the first time… I shared my *ONE MINUTE WITNESS* with him. And do you know what happened? He not only listened, but when I asked him, "What would hinder you from surrendering your life to Christ today?" he answered "nothing!" So he and I joined hands as he prayed to give his life to Jesus! It was unbelievable!

My harried lifestyle almost missed the best part of my day! And God used that stupid ice cream malt to get my attention! I am very glad He did.

Everyday we meet people who are ready to give their lives to

Christ. When we are looking for opportunities, we will find them. Even Jesus said,

"Do you not say, 'There are still four months and *then* comes the harvest'? Behold, I say to you, lift up your eyes and look at the fields, for they are already white for harvest!" (John 4:35).

So how do I lead someone to Christ? How do I transition from sharing my *ONE MINUTE WITNESS* to asking them about their own spiritual journey?

It's simple. Here are four key questions to memorize. When you are done sharing your testimony, thank them for listening, and then ask these questions:

1. *How about you? Do you have any spiritual beliefs?*

2. *So, do you think you would go to heaven?*

3. *What were you taught… how does someone get into heaven?*

4. *May I share how the Bible says you can know you are going to heaven?*

Usually they will agree to continue listening. The key is to ask if you can proceed further, and not assume or pressure people into listening. Remember, when you treat people with respect, they want to listen to you.

So I continue by saying, "Here's how the Bible says you can know for certain you are ready for heaven. It's easy as '1, 2, 3 or 'A,B,C'!"

1. ADMIT I am a sinner. We have all sinned, right? And since heaven is a perfect place, we all have a big problem. None of us can get to heaven because our good works don't erase our bad works.

143

2. BELIEVE that only Jesus Christ can remove my sin by dying on the cross for my sin. And then He rose again to prove He is God!

3. CONFESS my sins to Jesus, and ask Him to forgive me. Ask Him to be the Lord and boss of my life from this day onward. And ask Him to help me turn away from my sin, and follow Him everyday for the rest of my life.

I continue by saying, "Do you understand this? Does this make sense to you?" If they say, "Yes," then I ask, "So what would hold you back from surrendering your life to Jesus Christ today?"

Many say "Nothing!" If so, I ask if I could pray with them. Often they will take my hand and pray with me right there.

Others aren't ready, and that's ok. Simply ask them to start reading the Bible, starting in the book of John.

And before you leave, give them a couple websites that can take them further in their spiritual quest. We recommend these two:

www.frostygrapes.com
~ this is our follow-up website

www.salvationpoem.com
~ this gives you a great song and much more

The key is to ask the four questions. Their answers will reveal a great deal about what they are trusting to get themselves to heaven... their good works, or Christ's good work on the cross!

16
WIN-WIN APPLICATIONS
THAT TRANSFORM CHURCHES

I'm tired of *dead religion*; aren't you? When people go to church, many act like they are going to a funeral. They are always watching the clock, judging every song to see if they like the style of music, analyzing the preacher as if he's supposed to hit a home-run every time he's at bat, and telling God they will give in the offering... next week. But next week rarely comes. The announcements take almost as much time as the sermon, and the altars are rarely used. Pastor's grow tired of "dry altars" where no one responds, so he rarely calls people to spend extended times in prayer. And rarely do people get saved. People arrive fashionably late to service, and can't wait to get home to watch the game or go to their favorite restaurant. What's the problem?

We're overfed... and under-used. We've forgotten the reason we eat is so we can have energy to give out. We want to hire someone else to "Go into all the world and preach the gospel. It's just so much easier that way. Very few Christians share their faith, and many have trouble keeping a disciplined life of Bible reading and prayer.

But wait, when you hang around people who are in love with Jesus, everything looks different! Why? One word... Application. When I use what I learn, then I have better retention, and greater fruitfulness. Sharing my faith becomes a great adventure. My spirit comes alive when I give my faith away! When I don't, I become like the Dead Sea... all input and no output. And that, my friend, is a recipe for spiritual boredom, and ultimately, dead religion.

This is where the rubber meets the road. If I only learn theory in the church, and it all stays within the church, then how does the teaching help those who really need to hear? As the word says, "And how shall they believe in Him of whom they have not heard?" (Romans 10:14). Here are my favorite applications for our *ONE MINUTE WITNESS* tool:

CERTIFIED TRAINERS (CTs)

In many countries, hundreds of people are being trained to become Certified Trainers at our 5 Star Evangelism Seminar. This includes the equipping and application of the *ONE MINUTE WITNESS* tool. Pastors and evangelists are finding new hope and life through this seminar. Entire countries are being targeted through their denominational leaders and pastor's league presidents. Christians are finding a new excitement!

We train two Certified Trainers for every six churches. These CTs volunteer their time for a year to train all six of their assigned churches. Through these CTs, we are targeting a whole country, with a goal of training every willing Christian to share their faith compassionately and confidently. Through these trainers, churches are growing again. The people have a new fire for God as they successfully share their faith. Thousands are being saved. And God is glorified.

Our goal is to train Certified Trainers wherever God opens the door. Perhaps your denomination, pastor's association, church or youth group would be interested. To find out more, go to our website, www.oasisworldministries.org/certified-trainers.

At the end of this book, you will find a worksheet you can feel free to duplicate for the *ONE MINUTE WITNESS* training. Use it and spread it around. Just print our website on it so others can learn more too.

Pastor Samuel has a church of 500 in Mumbai, India. He decided to train his whole church in the *ONE MINUTE WITNESS*, and told them they should share their faith daily. And do you know what happened? Within two months, he had 100 new people attending his church!

Pastor Karl in Haiti testifies his church has grown by 300 people since we introduced the training of our *ONE MINUTE WITNESS*.

We have now printed this same, simple tool, *ONE MINUTE WITNESS* in 17 languages. Thousands are being trained by our Certified Trainers around the world. Pastors are excited to have a personal tool to equip their people… a tool that really works! And thousands are receiving Christ as their Lord, boss and owner.

Your ministry could change forever as you experience the exhilaration of sharing your faith, and then training others to do it too!

GAS BUY-DOWN

You've got to try this outreach! You will be amazed at the fun, equipping and great community PR your church group will receive.

This involves "buying down" the gas price by 25c/gallon for two hours on a Saturday. Your group has two hours of training and practice on the *ONE MINUTE WITNESS* tool, then we service all the pumps at a gas station for two hours. Kids are holding signs on the sidewalks, and within a few minutes you will have cars waiting in line. People will ask, "why are you doing this?" We tell them we are trying to show the love of God in a practical way... no strings attached. We offer to pump it for them, and wash their windows while they are waiting. Sometimes we offer free donuts and coffee while people are waiting in line. While their gas is being pumped, we say, "Sir, we're asking everyone the question of the day. Is that okay with you?" (he always responds affirmatively... after all he's getting free gas!) Then we ask, "what would you say is the best thing that has ever happened to you?"
People love the question, and often repeat it back as they are thinking about it. When they are done answering, we then ask, "May I share with you the best thing that has ever happened to me?" They say yes. And we share our testimony story for about one minute. About then their tank is full, so we thank them for participating, and tell them they can go inside to get their discount when they pay.

Your people will feel scared to death when they drive to the station; But when they leave after 2 hours of sharing their faith in a win-win situation, they feel *pumped!* They are so excited, and are willing to try sharing their faith again soon.

The main goal of this outreach is to equip your people to share their faith confidently. This will give them a great and easy tool, plus it will give them a window of practice together as a group in a positive environment. It's a WIN-WIN-WIN! The customers are happy, the station owner has done record business for two hours, and the Christians have found a new excitement in sharing their faith personally!

Upon completion of a Gas Buydown, one church member said, "I could not believe how easy it was to share my faith. I'm taking the challenge to doing this everyday for the next 21 days."

For more information on this great training outreach, go to www.gasbuydown.org.

PERSONAL IMPROMPTU SHARING

One size *really does* fit all with this tool. You can talk to well-known friends, workmates or even perfect strangers as you strike up a conversation. It works! If you don't believe me, try it! I have used this tool with perfect strangers hundreds of times. Without knowing who I am or anything about me, they start opening up their life story. People are longing to talk about significant stuff, not just the fluffy trivialities. Just try it at least four times. I guarantee you will be amazed at the openness of people.

Where could I use it? I just used it in the Chicago O'Hare airport at a kiosk where I was buying something. The worker was a Christian already, and it encouraged her when she saw other people sharing their faith. You could use this tool with strangers on the street as you do a community survey, you could do it when you hand out water bottles at a race, or when a plumber comes to fix something at your house. Every person you see has a soul... an eternal future. Wherever you find people, you have opportunities to use this tool. Remember, when you ask permission, it opens up a great window of opportunity.

I was flying home from a meeting, and didn't really *feel* like talking to anyone. Do you ever have those moments? Anyway, by the time we landed, the guy next to me started talking. So I joined in, and shared my *ONE MINUTE WITNESS*. Do you know what he said? "I have neglected the spiritual area in my life. You are right, I need to focus on this more. Thanks for talking to me." Well, I was sure glad I didn't follow my feelings. They will often lead us astray. Let's face it; our flesh will rarely lead us to share about Christ. Often we don't *feel led*, so let's pray for opportunities. If you are looking for them, you will find them everyday!

Bruce Schoeman tells people, "If you can read… you can lead… people to Christ." He has led many people to Christ simply by sharing Billy Graham's *Steps To Peace With God* tract. In other words, we can all be His witness by introducing a salvation tract to someone.

MORE OPPORTUNITIES

Marketplace Evangelism
I heard a pastor share that his congregation looks for people in need.
A couple from his church saw two women signing in deaf language, so they stopped, and asked if they could pray for a healing for her ear. She accepted… and God opened her ear! Is this going to happen every time I pray? Probably not, but as one pastor said, "We used to never pray for the sick, and we never saw people healed. Now we pray for the sick, and we are seeing people healed."

Why not ask God for miracles in the marketplace? Jesus used signs and wonders to draw attention to His power, and to provide practical relief for hurting people. This is normal, Biblical Christianity. Signs and wonders are very evangelistic! When I am in

India, people often approach our team, desperately look for healing through prayer. By God's grace, we see tremendous miracles on a regular basis. When in India we regularly see blind eyes healed, deaf ears opened, and numbness, back pain, and arthritis gone in the name of Jesus. Again, we are not the healer, but Jesus is. We tend to take responsibility for what only God can do. Our job is to pray in faith... God's job is to heal.

I asked a college student if he was Hindu. He said he was until last night. I asked what had happened last night? He told about the healing he saw in our Festival. The man everyone in town knew as the "town's blind man" was now seeing his wife for the first time in fifteen years. The college student remarked, "That's the kind of God I want to serve!"

If your neighbor needs help shoveling snow, or moving, or whatever- it's a great opportunity to put the love of God on display. My pastor friend, Clarence St. John, told his 80-year-old neighbor that he was personally going to be responsible for shoveling the snow off his driveway all winter. And in Minnesota, we have snow on the ground for at least five months of the year! To complicate it, Pastor Clarence travels a lot. But he made sure he always had a replacement person ready to shovel when he needed to travel. Do you think this 80-year-old man will be open to hearing the gospel someday?

Here is Paul's daily normal: "Therefore he reasoned in the synagogue with the Jews and with the *Gentile* worshipers, and in the marketplace daily with those who happened to be there" (Acts 17:17).

FRIENDSHIP EVANGELISM
We will never really know our neighbor's needs until we start

engaging them in conversation. Jesus was a "friend of sinners." So let's not be afraid of getting our hands dirty. Most lasting spiritual fruit is built upon relationships. And it's easier and more fun than you think! Here are some simple, yet effective ideas:

- Invite people over for a BBQ.

- Start a neighborhood crime watch. This is a great reason to knock on all your neighbor's doors and get their current names, phone numbers and emails for a directory.

- Host a holiday open house around Thanksgiving. Invite a couple neighbors to host it with you, and invite everyone to drop in as they can during an afternoon. People will love it.

- Start a backyard Bible club for children. Make it a one week event where your neighbors know you will be teaching them Bible stories that encourage children to honor their parents, to love at all times, and to honor God.

- Start a neighborhood Bible study.

- Start a "get out of debt seminar" at your church or local library community room.

This is worth repeating... "People won't care how much we know, until they know how much we care."

In India and other eastern countries, home care groups flourish. Here is their method: Prayer, Care, Share!
1. Start praying and fasting for your neighbor.
2. Do a "care act." In other words, show some kind of loving action to your neighbor.
3. Look for the opportunity to share your faith.

SPIRIT-PROMPTED SHARING

I knew of a man who would go out into the city's entertainment district on weekend nights, and just look at people, waiting for God to put someone on his heart. When he felt a surge of compassion for a certain person he saw, he would approach them and attempt to converse with them. What happened? He had great results!

Another group prayed God would give them a picture of someone in their mind, and then give them an appropriate word to share with them. After prayer they went out into the marketplace, and started interacting with these people as they saw them. They told them, "God has put you on my heart today. May I share with you what He told me?" They shared and prayed with 150 people to receive Jesus.

Just last night (as I am writing this), my wife and I were sitting with a salesman. Almost immediately I had a 'desire' to use our 'One Minute Witness' tool with him. So when we were finished talking about our business at hand, I said: "Unrelated to our business today, I wonder if could ask you an interesting question? Would that be OK with you?" From there he began to say that the best thing that had ever happened to him was that he was now sober for seven months. He said it without hesitating, and he said it with pride. He told us how his life had hit rock-bottom, and that he had lost everything. But his life was now taking a turn, and he was happy for it.

Imagine, a total stranger bearing his soul. When it's a God-thing, you will be amazed at how people respond. I then told him how Jesus had totally changed my life.

How do I begin? Simply pray God will soften your heart and divinely direct you to someone in need today. Tomorrow never comes. I think it's called being *Spirit-led!* It might be a little scary at times, but it sure is fun to look back and see what God did!

So, are you ready for a challenge? Let's get out of the church... out of our comfort zone... out of dead religiosity... out of Phariseeism... out of the salt-shaker... and into the world! And let's do it together...

17

FOR SERIOUS EYES ONLY

Has God ever *double-dared* you? He did me! Years ago God talked to me about sharing my faith more often. He seemed to ask me some very probing questions:

> – *Are you really serious about sharing your faith?*
> *Or are you just satisfied where you are?*
> – *Do you want to go the next level?*
> – *Do you really believe in a heaven and hell?*
> – *Do you really want to "surrender all?"*
> – *Do you really want to fulfill My purpose for your life?*

So I took the challenge from the Holy Spirit to share my faith with someone every day for seven days. I know it sounds like a small goal. But for me it was a big goal. I do not want to fail the Lord with what I vow to Him. I thought, *"Can I really do this?... and furthermore, will I do this?"*

But as I told you earlier, I shared with eleven people in seven days. It was amazing to see how open people were. When I was a pastor of a church, I thought most people were not open to hear the gospel. After all, most churches were not growing.

But I was absolutely wrong. Ninety-five percent of the people I share with are open. Everyone is looking for purpose and hope. I am still utterly surprised how people listen, and many times are ready to give their lives to Jesus Christ on the spot!

And did I say I was having fun? Absolutely... I've never had more fun as a Christian than when I can be a part of something eternal. And you can too! Just train, ask and offer your daily availability. The second chapter of Acts did not say when the Holy Spirit comes that you will *"go witnessing"* for a weekend or two. It clearly says, "you will be my witnesses." I am no Greek scholar, but the Greek word for *"witnesses"* is *"martyress."* It is where we get our English word *"martyr."* It's interesting that all eleven disciples fled when Jesus was arrested in the garden of Gethsemane. But all of the same disciples became literal martyrs for Christ, except John, who was exiled on the island of Patmos for the rest of his life.

What was the difference?

They were filled with the Holy Spirit. This was the turning point for them. And it is for us today too.

Every day they shared their own stories about Jesus with new passion, and with much less fear of man. They were thrown in jail, beaten, heckled... and killed. And they "turned the world upside down" for Christ (Acts 17:6).

On September 11, 2001, eighteen men turned the world upside

down. Eighteen men who loved not their lives unto death decided to master-plan a strategy to fly planes into the World Trade Center in New York City, killing themselves and 3,000 others. Since that day, life has never been the same.

Kamikaze pilots fearlessly flew over Pearl Harbor, knowing they probably would not return. They counted the cost, and found their cause was worthy of their very lives.

Middle East radicals are trained to strap bombs to their waists and set them off in crowded areas. They are each promised 70 brown-eyed virgins in heaven. Their mother's actually rejoice that their family could offer one of their children as a martyr. You may not have to literally die for your Christian faith, although I am told that around 350 people do each day. But can we choose right now to die to our own selfishness, our independence and our apathy? Can we choose to believe that today is the day of salvation?

Our world is a different world today. Times are changing. In most areas of the world the gospel of Jesus Christ is spreading rapidly. In North America and Europe, it is not. We are not unlike the children of Israel in the Old Testament of the Bible. When they obeyed God humbly, God blessed them abundantly. But soon their blessings became their curse, as the next generation forgot Who had blessed them... and why.

So what will happen? Our fate is in our hands... and our feet... and our mouths.

I want to challenge you boldly today. Will you become an everyday witness? Will you pray for daily opportunities to sow the gospel into people's lives who are ready to receive? Will you allow the Holy Spirit to empower you to be His martyr? His witness? Will you try it for seven days? For twenty-one days? (I am told research shows twenty-one days makes a habit.)

I double-dare you!
It helped me a lot to do two important things:

1. Have someone else take the challenge with me.

2. Write down my results on a calendar each day.
   Our website can help keep you motivated.

If you'll take the dare, contact a partner and ask them to try it with you for seven days, then twenty-one days. You'll be glad you did.

Take a challenge that will turn your world upside down. People's souls are hanging in the balance, waiting for you to "tell them what great things the Lord has done for you" (Mark 5:19).

The apostle Paul is in prison, having been beat up and tortured because of his faith. Yet he realizes his mission field is wherever he happens to be. Listen with me to his closing prayer in Ephesians 6:19-20:

> "And [pray] for me, that utterance may be given to me, that I may open my mouth boldly to make known the mystery of the gospel, for which I am an ambassador in chains; that in it I may speak boldly, as I ought to speak."

When I was twelve years old, I remember lying in bed listening to my radio as the Christian station was signing off each night at 10pm. Every night they would play the same song. I have to admit, the lyrics both challenged me to do better, and sort of haunted me at the same time.

Lyrics: Ensign Edwin Young
Music: Harry E. Storrs

"I wonder have I done my best for Jesus,   Who died upon the cruel tree?   To think of His great sacrifice at Calvary! I know my Lord expects the best from me.

How many are the lost that I have lifted?   How many are the chained I've helped to free? I wonder, have I done my best for Jesus,   when He has done so much for me?"

Maybe it sounds a little condemning to our *feel-good* generation. But to me it wasn't. It was challenging me in a good way to stay focused. And I am grateful for the memory of that song. It still challenges me today.

CLOSING WORDS

"If we aim for heaven, the earth will be given to us. If we aim for earth we will obtain neither." C.S. Lewis

Do you know what makes God smile?

Prayer and Bible reading? Church attendance? Good works? I'm sure they are in Heaven's top ten. But what does the Bible specifically mention that prompts a party in heaven?

In Luke 15 we are told that all the angels in Heaven rejoice over one sinner that repents. This rings the bells of Heaven! The ninety-nine that are already saved are important to God... but not as important as the one lost sheep. Do you want to bring a smile to God's face? Love lost sheep.

I am an evangelist. No, not a business evangelist or a technical evangelist, as many companies label their specialists today. "Evangel" means *good news*. Thus, I am the bearer of good news! As an evangelist, I equip others to share the good news.

I believe you and I have the greatest job on earth. No, not being an evangelist, or a plumber or a nurse, or whatever your job is, but being an ambassador for Jesus Christ! To be the president of my country would be a demotion. I get to influence lives for eternity! I get to offer people hope and purpose! I get to make a difference in the here and now! I get to represent the King of all kings who ever lived throughout all history!

There is no better news than to know our lives have an eternal purpose and meaning. It is good news that my past sins are really forgiven and forgotten. But this good news is bottlenecked inside our churches. And most unbelievers won't visit our churches. So, I have two questions for you.

1. How many people have ever shared with you about their love for Jesus, outside of any religious events? A few? One? No one? Most people I ask say no one has ever witnessed to me personally about how Jesus has changed their life.

2. Would you like to do better at representing the tremendous love of Jesus to the people in your world? Most people I ask respond with an immediate "Yes!"

Some days I am a better witness for my Lord than others. Some days I forget all about the pre-believers around me. But it doesn't bother me anymore, because I have decided to follow Jesus. There's no more condemnation. Why? God sees my heart, and I have started down a road of no return. I will be His witness. I can never be satisfied with anything less. Now, sharing my faith brings new excitement everyday to my life. I'm not perfect. I'm still learning. But it's life's great adventure! And it's scary fun!

Will you join me? I mean really, will you join me? Go to our website now... www.oneminutewitness.org. By God's grace, we will be His everyday witnesses on this earth. And someday we will meet in Heaven and share life's greatest joy... sharing Christ with others!

Question to ponder:

"Many believers wait until the last two weeks of their life–when death is imminent–before they start sharing their faith and talking to friends and family. Will you wait that long?" ~Bruce Schoeman

Action point:

Will you write down three people you would like to share Christ with in the next 30 days? Start praying daily for them, and watch for the opportunity!

1. _____

2. _____

3. _____

18

BEFORE WE FINISH...

HOW TO AVOID THE 6 DEADLY SINS OF EVANGELISM

Congratulations for finishing the book! As we bring this to a close, I am praying it will be a fresh beginning for you. Here's six "don'ts" that will help you finish strong. God is with you!

1. DON'T LOSE FOCUS.

One pastor said, *"We don't fall out of love, we fall out of focus."* Desire follows focus. We all desire to see the world evangelized, but our desire may be lower than it used to be because we are focused on too many other priorities. A person can only have so many focuses. I wrote a song called *Back To The Basics.* The lyrics highlight four basics upon which we should stay focused...

"Love my Bible, praise each day, help the downcast, share my faith."

If I can keep my spiritual life focused on just these four things, I will grow steadily. If not, my growth will be stunted. Jesus gave us two things upon which we should focus... Love God. Love People. But too often we start loving *things*, and then our lives get really messed up.

I thought most people in my country were not open to hear the gospel, because most churches were not growing. But I was totally wrong! When I started engaging people politely with my testimony, I found 95% were very open. Barna Research shows that 75% of Americans are open to hearing a faith story from someone they trust. Everyone needs hope, and we have it. But we've just lost our Great Commission focus.

However, when we focus on sharing our faith, fresh creativity begins to arise. When we actually start to share our faith, instead of just preaching, teaching, praying, singing and talking about it, desire begins to be birthed again. And do you know what else happens?

– Compassion arises.

– Creativity multiplies.

– Confidence is restored.

– And Christ smiles.

Inspiration delayed is often inspiration lost. So when God starts tugging at your heart, don't tell Him to wait.

When He gives you the nudge, seize the moment! Share your faith! Focus is your friend. Sometimes feelings are not.

Remember, practice makes perfect. Everyday when I came home from school, my mom insisted I practice piano for thirty minutes every day! It almost killed me, especially when my friends were all playing football in my yard! But her disciplined approach benefited me greatly. The more you apply yourself, the better you can become.

Go ahead and do it! Share your faith!

2. DON'T WATER DOWN THE GOSPEL.

We all know love wins, so everyone goes to heaven, right? Let's face it, no one wants to talk about hell. So should we misrepresent it or change what the Bible says about it, or avoid it altogether? Should we agree with our culture that says "all roads lead to God" as if Jesus is just one of many ways? Should we be silent when our friends say they need to find their own way to God? Should we just take our ball and go home, thinking there's no hope of God ever using me?

Let's put on our big-boy pants. Not everyone is going to agree with us. To some, the gospel will be an offense. To others it will be a life-preserver (2 Corinthians 2:15-16). It is not up to us to change the message. We are simply here to *deliver* the message... in love. I don't need to apologize for what I don't understand. And I don't need to have all the answers. If I did, I would be God.

People don't understand everything about their car engine, but they depend on it because it works. I don't understand all of God's ways, but I depend on it, along with hundreds of millions of others, because it heals, protects and restores my purpose in life. It works! The Bible says, "true and righteous are Your judgments" (Revelation 16:7), so I leave the judgments up to Him. My job is simply to point people to the Jesus of the Bible... to the Jesus who changed my life... to the Jesus I love more than anything or anyone else... to the Jesus who loves me unconditionally.

3. DON'T OVER-COMPLICATE THE GOSPEL.

Another deadly sin is to forget this gospel is so simple a child can understand it.

A five-year-old kid never starts in seventh grade. He starts in kindergarten. When sharing our faith, people don't have to know or hear all the doctrines of your church. They won't listen to you if you won't stop talking long enough to take a breath and listen to them. And they certainly won't know all the meanings of our "Christianese" language we are accustomed to. Remember, it's never about saying exactly the right words. People sense what's in your heart, and the Holy Spirit has already been speaking to them.

Some don't understand salvation is a free gift. Others think I need to keep confessing all my old sins. Many think if my good works are more than my bad works, then I will go to heaven. But the Holy Spirit will help you know what to say. Don't be afraid to speak the truth in love. If Jesus said you have to become like a child to enter the kingdom of heaven, I would guess He also meant a child could understand how to be forgiven.

The gospel is simple as 1-2-3.

1. I am a sinner, and my efforts to be good aren't good enough.

2. Jesus died in my place, and rose again, proving He was the real Savior.

3. I must choose 24/7 to turn from my wrongs, and make Him the Lord (boss) of my life.

Again, the gospel is simple as A-B-C.

A—I must ADMIT I am a sinner, and I cannot get to heaven by myself.

B—I must BELIEVE only Jesus dying for my sin can save me. My good works don't erase my bad works, but His death and resurrection can.

C—I must CONFESS my sins and ask Jesus to forgive me and be the only leader of my life from here on out.

Learn to share Jesus concisely, precisely and clearly. That's right, *learn* to share your faith-story. It doesn't always come naturally. But once you know it, your fears of not knowing what to say will disappear, and you will find great joy in sharing. More importantly, they will find hope while listening to you.

God will also teach you to act on His promptings, and not follow your own feelings. Feelings are not always our friend. Often you will begin sharing your faith... by faith. You won't feel any leading. You will just learn to recognize an opportunity. And once you begin to act on the opportunity, it can be absolutely exhilarating to see what God does through you. Being filled with and led by the Holy Spirit on a daily basis is one of life's great joys!

4. DON'T MAKE IT VAGUE.

No one watches black-and-white television anymore. Instead, tell your personal story in full and living color. From God's perspective, your coming to Christ is exciting and worth sharing! Learn to share it from your heart. Www.oneminutewitness.org provides a template to help you share your testimony. The moment you start sharing from your heart, and not just from your head, people will listen. The best advertising today is a person's testimonial. One of your best tools is your testimony. Ask them if you can share the best thing that has ever happened to you. Asking shows respect. Make the gospel personal, colorful and delightful, because Jesus loves people... *deeply!*

5. DON'T FORGET TO FOLLOW-THROUGH.

We can lose our harvest on this one.

James said, "you do not have because you do not ask" (James 4:2). There are two things that are crucial to ask someone when sharing your faith. First, if they seem interested, ask if they would like to pray to receive Jesus as the leader of their life. If you sense they are not ready, don't push it. You are still a success if you help them come one step closer to yielding to Christ. One sows, another reaps.

Clarence St. John talks about the road to Jesus:
"All people are on a 20 point span:
Worst person is a -10.
Best person is a +10.
Wherever you find them, just bump them up a notch."

Tom Trazinski makes the wonderful point, "Where did evangelism happen along that 20 point scale? All the way!"

In other words, if I can help bring them one step closer to Christ, it's a win!

Second, ask if you can get together (or call them) in the next day or two to pray with them about things they care about. If I never ask, I will never know if they want to go further. Some people are ready now, and others don't know they are ready. So plan for another contact. If they prayed to receive Christ, don't abandon them. Give them a call. Give them a tract. Give them a website that will help them grow (www.frostygrapes. com). Give them a good church near their home. But best of all, give them some more of your time in an atmosphere that doesn't spook them. Be their friend.

After describing a product, a successful salesman will either ask for the sale, or schedule another time to talk, or both. Stay in touch with people, whether they accept Christ on the spot or not. Jesus was a friend of sinners. But don't take their "no" as a personal rejection. When you respectfully tell them your story, you win.

Here's two winning questions that will help you do the ask with confidence:

1. What would hinder you from surrendering your life to Jesus Christ right now?

2. Can you think of a better time than right now to ask Christ into your life?

Here's a couple more great follow-up websites to which you can refer people:

www.frostygrapes.com
www.salvationpoem.com

6. DON'T FORGET TO CELEBRATE WINS!

The angels celebrate, so why shouldn't we? In fact, according to Luke 15, "all heaven" celebrates when just one sinner repents! We celebrate sports, graduations, anniversaries and birthdays. Why not invite a few friends to meet for dessert and introduce the one you recently led to Christ? It will affirm the new believer, and it will encourage your friends that if God can use you, He can use anybody!

But we should also feel good about how God uses us. Thank Him for anointing you. Brag (a little) about how God worked through you. Let your confidence grow. Give Him the glory, and ask Him to do it again... soon. Tell Him you are available again tomorrow.

Feel His pleasure and His smile. Savor the moment. Heaven does!

And here is a suggested prayer you can ask them to repeat:

"Dear Jesus,
I admit I am a sinner. I am sorry for the wrong I've done. I believe
You died for my sin, and rose again. I confess my sins, and ask
You to forgive me right now. Help me to turn away from what You
call sin, and to follow Your ways. I give You my heart and my life
forever. I love You Jesus, and I thank You. Amen."

When you are finished praying, ask them, "What happened in your life when you prayed?" They often say they are experiencing new peace or they feel good. Congratulate them, and encourage them that they made the right choice. I tell them there are three things that will help them be a strong follower of Jesus...

1. Read your Bible and pray everyday.

2. Find a Bible-believing church, and attend every Sunday.

3. Tell the pastor and other people that you gave your heart to Jesus.

Ask for their phone and email, and ask if you could call them tomorrow and share one of your favorite scriptures with them. Be sure to call within 24 hours. After that, try to keep connecting, or find someone in their area that could connect with them.

And be encouraged. All the angels in heaven are rejoicing with you! (Luke 15).

LET'S FINISH IN PRAYER

PRAYER #1-Here's a sample prayer you could use in leading someone into a relationship with Jesus Christ. Ask them to repeat it after you.

> *"Dear Jesus,*
> *I admit I am a sinner. I am sorry for my sins. I believe You died for my wrong, and rose again from the dead. I confess my sins right now, and I ask You to forgive me. Make me clean inside. I give You my heart, and ask You to be the Lord and boss of my life forever. I love you Jesus, and I receive Your great love. Amen."*

PRAYER #2 – Here's my prayer for both you and I…

> *"Dear Lord,*
> *I am so grateful someone shared Your love with me. I love You so much. From this moment on, please help me to love people with Your love. Open my eyes to the hurting people all around me each day. Help me to learn to share my faith effectively with compassion and confidence. My life belongs to You. I am available to be Your witness today! In Jesus' mighty name I pray, amen."*

I am praying you will have a fresh beginning. God is training up a mighty army to compassionately and confidently share their faith in Jesus Christ. You are now recruited! Now it's time for some *scary fun!*

To receive Tom's One Minute Witness e-mail or join our prayer-partners E-mail list, and to learn about the great harvest we are experiencing, go to www.oasisworldministries.org.

Additional Ministry Weblinks

5StarEvangelism.org (Seminar & Trainers program info)
EvangelistsRoundtable.com (U.S. Roundtables details)
FrostyGrapes.com (A leave-behind, follow-up Website)
GasBuyDown.org (An effective team outreach)
iRepentNetwork.org (Twin Cities prayer initiative)
OasisInternational.org (Water wells info)
OneMinuteWitness.org (Evangelism tool)

My Favorite New Testament Evangelism Verses

Then He said to them, "Follow Me, and I will make you fishers of men." They immediately left *their* nets and followed Him. (Matthew 4:19, 20)

"You are the light of the world. A city that is set on a hill cannot be hidden. "Nor do they light a lamp and put it under a basket, but on a lampstand, and it gives light to all *who are* in the house. "Let your light so shine before men, that they may see your good works and glorify your Father in heaven. (Matthew 5:14-16)

"Not everyone who says to Me, 'Lord, Lord,' shall enter the kingdom of heaven, but he who does the will of My Father in heaven. (Matthew 7:21)

But when He saw the multitudes, He was moved with compassion for them, because they were weary and scattered, like sheep having no shepherd. Then He said to His disciples, "The harvest truly *is* plentiful, but the laborers are few. "Therefore pray the Lord of the harvest to send out laborers into His harvest." (Matthew 9:36-38)

For what profit is it to a man if he gains the whole world, and loses his own soul? Or what will a man give in exchange for his soul? (Matthew 16:26)

"For the Son of Man has come to save that which was lost. (Matthew 18:11)

'Therefore go into the highways, and as many as you find, invite to the wedding.' (Matthew 22:9)

"O Jerusalem, Jerusalem, the one who kills the prophets and stones those who are sent to her! How often I wanted to gather your children together, as a hen gathers her chicks under *her* wings, but you were not willing! (Matthew 23:37)

"And this gospel of the kingdom will be preached in all the world as a witness to all the nations, and then the end will come. (Matthew 24:14)

"Watch therefore, for you know neither the day nor the hour in which the Son of Man is coming. (Matthew 25:13)

So they went out quickly from the tomb with fear and great joy, and ran to bring His disciples word. "Go therefore and make disciples of all the nations, baptizing them in the name of the Father and of the Son and of the Holy Spirit, "teaching them to observe all things that I have commanded you; and lo, I am with you always, *even* to the end of the age." Amen. (Matthew 28:8, 19, 20)

When Jesus heard *it*, He said to them, "Those who are well have no need of a physician, but those who are sick. I did not come to call *the* righteous, but sinners, to repentance." (Mark 2:17)

"But these are the ones sown on good ground, those who hear the word, accept *it*, and bear fruit: some thirtyfold, some sixty, and some a hundred." (Mark 4:20)

And when He got into the boat, he *who had been* demon-possessed begged Him that he might be with Him. However, Jesus did not permit him, but said to him, "Go home to your friends, and tell them what great things the Lord has done for you, and how He has had compassion on you." And he departed and began to proclaim in Decapolis all that Jesus had done for him; and all marveled. (Mark 5:18-20)

And He called the twelve to *Himself*, and began to send them out two *by* two, and gave them power over unclean spirits. (Mark 6:7)

Then the veil of the temple was torn in two from top to bottom. Joseph of Arimathea, a prominent council member, who was himself waiting for the kingdom of God, coming and taking courage, went in to Pilate and asked for the body of Jesus. (Mark 15:38, 43)

And He said to them, "Go into all the world and preach the gospel to every creature. [...] And they went out and preached everywhere, the Lord working with *them* and confirming the word through the accompanying signs. Amen. (Mark 16:15, 20)

"The Spirit of the LORD is upon Me,
Because He has anointed Me
To preach the gospel to the poor;
He has sent Me to heal the brokenhearted,
To proclaim liberty to the captives
And recovery of sight to the blind,
To set at liberty those who are oppressed;
To proclaim the acceptable year of the LORD."
but He said to them, "I must preach the kingdom of God to the other cities also, because for this purpose I have been sent." (Luke 4:18, 19, 43)

For he and all who were with him were astonished at the catch of fish which they had taken; and so also *were* James and John, the sons of Zebedee, who were partners with Simon. And Jesus said to Simon, "Do not be afraid. From now on you will catch men." "I have not come to call *the* righteous, but sinners, to repentance." (Luke 5:9, 10, 32)

Then He called His twelve disciples together and gave them power and authority over all demons, and to cure diseases. So they departed and went through the towns, preaching the gospel and healing everywhere. "For what profit is it to a man if he gains the whole world, and is himself destroyed or lost?" (Luke 9:1, 6, 25)

Then He said to them, "The harvest truly is great, but the laborers *are* few; therefore pray the Lord of the harvest to send out laborers into His harvest. (Luke 10:2)

Then one said to Him, "Lord, are there few who are saved?" And He said to them, "Strive to enter through the narrow gate, for many, I say to you, will seek to enter and will not be able. (Luke 13:23, 24)

Then the master said to the servant, 'Go out into the highways and hedges, and compel *them* to come in, that my house may be filled. (Luke 14:23)

"And when he comes home, he calls together *his* friends and neighbors, saying to them, 'Rejoice with me, for I have found my sheep which was lost!' "I say to you that likewise there will be more joy in heaven over one sinner who repents than over ninety-nine just persons who need no repentance. "Or what woman, having ten silver coins, if she loses one coin, does not light a lamp, sweep the house, and search carefully until she finds *it*? "And

when she has found *it*, she calls her friends and neighbors together, saying, 'Rejoice with me, for I have found the piece which I lost!' "Likewise, I say to you, there is joy in the presence of the angels of God over one sinner who repents."
(Luke 15:6-10)

"And he arose and came to his father. But when he was still a great way off, his father saw him and had compassion, and ran and fell on his neck and kissed him. "And the son said to him, 'Father, I have sinned against heaven and in your sight, and am no longer worthy to be called your son.' "But the father said to his servants, 'Bring out the best robe and put *it* on him, and put a ring on his hand and sandals on *his* feet. 'And bring the fatted calf here and kill *it*, and let us eat and be merry; 'for this my son was dead and is alive again; he was lost and is found.' And they began to be merry.
(Luke 15:20-24)

"So the master commended the unjust steward because he had dealt shrewdly. For the sons of this world are more shrewd in their generation than the sons of light." "And I say to you, make friends for yourselves by unrighteous mammon, that when you fail, they may receive you into an everlasting home. (Luke 16:8, 9)

"But he said to him, 'If they do not hear Moses and the prophets, neither will they be persuaded though one rise from the dead.' "
(Luke 16:31)

"Whoever seeks to save his life will lose it, and whoever loses his life will preserve it. "I tell you, in that night there will be two *men* in one bed: the one will be taken and the other will be left. Two *women* will be grinding together: the one will be taken and the other left. Two men will be in the field: the one will be taken and the other left." (Luke 17:33-36)

But Jesus called them to *Him* and said, "Let the little children come to Me, and do not forbid them; for of such is the kingdom of God. (Luke 18:16)

Now a certain ruler asked Him, saying, "Good Teacher, what shall I do to inherit eternal life?" (Luke 18:18)

"Whoever falls on that stone will be broken; but on whomever it falls, it will grind him to powder." (Luke 20:18)

"Now when these things begin to happen, look up and lift up your heads, because your redemption draws near." (Luke 21:28)

And Jesus said to him, "Assuredly, I say to you, today you will be with Me in Paradise." (Luke 23:43)

Then He said to them, "Thus it is written, and thus it was necessary for the Christ to suffer and to rise from the dead the third day, "and that repentance and remission of sins should be preached in His name to all nations, beginning at Jerusalem. (Luke 24:46, 47)

But as many as received Him, to them He gave the right to become children of God, to those who believe in His name: (John 1:12)

"For God so loved the world that He gave His only begotten Son, that whoever believes in Him should not perish but have everlasting life. "For God did not send His Son into the world to condemn the world, but that the world through Him might be saved. (John 3:16, 17)

The woman said to Him, "I know that Messiah is coming" (who is called Christ). "When He comes, He will tell us all things." Jesus said to her, "I who speak to you am *He*." (John 4:25, 26)

And many of the Samaritans of that city believed in Him because of the word of the woman who testified, "He told me all that I *ever* did." (John 4:39)

Then he inquired of them the hour when he got better. And they said to him, "Yesterday at the seventh hour the fever left him." So the father knew that *it was* at the same hour in which Jesus said to him, "Your son lives." And he himself believed, and his whole household. (John 4:52, 53)

"Most assuredly, I say to you, he who hears My word and believes in Him who sent Me has everlasting life, and shall not come into judgment, but has passed from death into life. (John 5:24)

And Jesus said to them, "I am the bread of life. He who comes to Me shall never hunger, and he who believes in Me shall never thirst. "And this is the will of Him who sent Me, that everyone who sees the Son and believes in Him may have everlasting life; and I will raise him up at the last day." (John 6:35, 40)

Then Jesus spoke to them again, saying, "I am the light of the world. He who follows Me shall not walk in darkness, but have the light of life." (John 8:12)

"And you shall know the truth, and the truth shall make you free." "Therefore if the Son makes you free, you shall be free indeed. (John 8:32, 36)

"I must work the works of Him who sent Me while it is day; *the* night is coming when no one can work. (John 9:4)

"I am the door. If anyone enters by Me, he will be saved, and will go in and out and find pasture. "The thief does not come except to steal, and to kill, and to destroy. I have come that they may have life, and that they may have *it* more abundantly. "I am the good shepherd; and I know My sheep, and am known by My own. (John 10:9, 10, 14)

"And I give them eternal life, and they shall never perish; neither shall anyone snatch them out of My hand. (John 10:28)

Jesus said to her, "I am the resurrection and the life. He who believes in Me, though he may die, he shall live. (John 11:25)

Then many of the Jews who had come to Mary, and had seen the things Jesus did, believed in Him. (John 11:45)

But the chief priests plotted to put Lazarus to death also, because on account of him many of the Jews went away and believed in Jesus. (John 12:10, 11)

"Now is the judgment of this world; now the ruler of this world will be cast out. "And I, if I am lifted up from the earth, will draw all *peoples* to Myself." (John 12:31, 32)

Jesus said to him, "I am the way, the truth, and the life. No one comes to the Father except through Me. (John 14:6)

Every branch in Me that does not bear fruit He takes away; and every *branch* that bears fruit He prunes, that it may bear more fruit. (John 15:2)

So Jesus said to them again, "Peace to you! As the Father has sent Me, I also send you." (John 20:21)

And truly Jesus did many other signs in the presence of His disciples, which are not written in this book; but these are written that you may believe that Jesus is the Christ, the Son of God, and that believing you may have life in His name. (John 20:30, 31)

And it shall come to pass
That whoever calls on the name of the LORD
Shall be saved.' (Acts 2:21)

And with many other words he testified and exhorted them, saying, "Be saved from this perverse generation." Then those who gladly received his word were baptized; and that day about three thousand souls were added *to them.* (Acts 2:40, 41)

For Moses truly said to the fathers, *'The LORD your God will raise up for you a Prophet like me from your brethren. Him you shall hear in all things, whatever He says to you.* (Acts 3:22)

However, many of those who heard the word believed; and the number of the men came to be about five thousand. (Acts 4:4)

"This is the *'stone which was rejected by you builders, which has become the chief cornerstone.'* "Nor is there salvation in any other, for there is no other name under heaven given among men by which we must be saved." (Acts 4:11, 12)

"Now, Lord, look on their threats, and grant to Your servants that with all boldness they may speak Your word, "by stretching out Your hand to heal, and that signs and wonders may be done through the name of Your holy Servant Jesus." And when they had prayed, the place where they were assembled together was shaken; and they were all filled with the Holy Spirit, and they spoke the word of God with boldness. (Acts 4:29-31)

And believers were increasingly added to the Lord, multitudes of both men and women, (Acts 5:14)

"Go, stand in the temple and speak to the people all the words of this life." (Acts 5:20)

And daily in the temple, and in every house, they did not cease teaching and preaching Jesus *as* the Christ. (Acts 5:42)

Then the word of God spread, and the number of the disciples multiplied greatly in Jerusalem, and a great many of the priests were obedient to the faith. (Acts 6:7)

Now an angel of the Lord spoke to Philip, saying, "Arise and go toward the south along the road which goes down from Jerusalem to Gaza." This is desert. Then Philip said, "If you believe with all your heart, you may." And he answered and said, "I believe that Jesus Christ is the Son of God." So he commanded the chariot to stand still. And both Philip and the eunuch went down into the water, and he baptized him. (Acts 8:26, 37, 38)

But the Lord said to him, "Go, for he is a chosen vessel of Mine to bear My name before Gentiles, kings, and the children of Israel. (Acts 9:15)

Now it came to pass, as Peter went through all *parts of the country*, that he also came down to the saints who dwelt in Lydda. So all who dwelt at Lydda and Sharon saw him and turned to the Lord. [...] Then Peter arose and went with them. When he had come, they brought *him* to the upper room. And all the widows stood by him weeping, showing the tunics and garments which Dorcas had made while she was with them. But Peter put them all out, and knelt down and prayed. And turning to the body he said, "Tabitha, arise."

And she opened her eyes, and when she saw Peter she sat up. And it became known throughout all Joppa, and many believed on the Lord. (Acts 9:32, 35, 39, 40, 42)

Now those who were scattered after the persecution that arose over Stephen traveled as far as Phoenicia, Cyprus, and Antioch, preaching the word to no one but the Jews only. And the hand of the Lord was with them, and a great number believed and turned to the Lord. (Acts 11:19, 21)

Then the proconsul believed, when he saw what had been done, being astonished at the teaching of the Lord.
(Acts 13:12)

"For so the Lord has commanded us: *'I have set you as a light to the Gentiles, That you should be for salvation to the ends of the earth.'* " Now when the Gentiles heard this, they were glad and glorified the word of the Lord. And as many as had been appointed to eternal life believed. (Acts 13:47, 48)

Therefore they stayed there a long time, speaking boldly in the Lord, who was bearing witness to the word of His grace, granting signs and wonders to be done by their hands.
(Acts 14:3)

And when they had preached the gospel to that city and made many disciples, they returned to Lystra, Iconium, and Antioch,
(Acts 14:21)

"But we believe that through the grace of the Lord Jesus Christ we shall be saved in the same manner as they."
'After this I will return And will rebuild the tabernacle of David, which has fallen down;
I will rebuild its ruins,
And I will set it up;
So that the rest of mankind may seek the LORD,
Even all the Gentiles who are called by My name,
Says the LORD who does all these things.' (Acts 15:11, 16, 17)

But when they did not find them, they dragged Jason and some brethren to the rulers of the city, crying out, "These who have turned the world upside down have come here too. [...] Therefore many of them believed, and also not a few of the Greeks, prominent women as well as men. (Acts 17:6, 12)

Therefore he reasoned in the synagogue with the Jews and with the *Gentile* worshipers, and in the marketplace daily with those who happened to be there. (Acts 17:17)

"And He has made from one blood every nation of men to dwell on all the face of the earth, and has determined their preappointed times and the boundaries of their dwellings, "so that they should seek the Lord, in the hope that they might grope for Him and find Him, though He is not far from each one of us; (Acts 17:26, 27)

And he went into the synagogue and spoke boldly for three months, reasoning and persuading concerning the things of the kingdom of God. But when some were hardened and did not believe, but spoke evil of the Way before the multitude, he departed from them and withdrew the disciples, reasoning daily in the school of Tyrannus. And this continued for two years, so that all who dwelt in Asia heard the word of the Lord Jesus, both Jews and Greeks. (Acts 19:8-10)

And many who had believed came confessing and telling their deeds. Also, many of those who had practiced magic brought their books together and burned *them* in the sight of all. And they counted up the value of them, and it totaled fifty thousand *pieces* of silver. So the word of the Lord grew mightily and prevailed. (Acts 19:18-20)

'But rise and stand on your feet; for I have appeared to you for this purpose, to make you a minister and a witness both of the things which you have seen and of the things which I will yet reveal to you. 'I will deliver you from the *Jewish* people, as well as *from* the Gentiles, to whom I now send you, 'to open their eyes, *in order* to turn *them* from darkness to light, and *from* the power of Satan to God, that they may receive forgiveness of sins and an inheritance among those who are sanctified by faith in Me.' (Acts 26:16-18)

"Therefore, King Agrippa, I was not disobedient to the heavenly vision, but declared first to those in Damascus and in Jerusalem, and throughout all the region of Judea, and *then* to the Gentiles, that they should repent, turn to God, and do works befitting repentance. (Acts 26:19, 20)

For I am not ashamed of the gospel of Christ, for it is the power of God to salvation for everyone who believes, for the Jew first and also for the Greek. (Romans 1:16)

For the wages of sin *is* death, but the gift of God *is* eternal life in Christ Jesus our Lord. (Romans 6:23)

The Spirit Himself bears witness with our spirit that we are children of God, (Romans 8:16)

Brethren, my heart's desire and prayer to God for Israel is that they may be saved. (Romans 10:1)

[...] that if you confess with your mouth the Lord Jesus and believe in your heart that God has raised Him from the dead, you will be saved. For with the heart one believes unto righteousness, and with the mouth confession is made unto salvation. (Romans 10:9, 10)

How then shall they call on Him in whom they have not believed? And how shall they believe in Him of whom they have not heard? And how shall they hear without a preacher? And how shall they preach unless they are sent? As it is written: *"How beautiful are the feet of those who preach the gospel of peace, Who bring glad tidings of good things!"* (Romans 10:14, 15)

For I speak to you Gentiles; inasmuch as I am an apostle to the Gentiles, I magnify my ministry, if by any means I may provoke to jealousy *those who are* my flesh and save some of them. (Romans 11:13, 14)

And so I have made it my aim to preach the gospel, not where Christ was named, lest I should build on another man's foundation, but as it is written: *"To whom He was not announced, they shall see; And those who have not heard shall understand."* (Romans 15:20, 21)

For the unbelieving husband is sanctified by the wife, and the unbelieving wife is sanctified by the husband; otherwise your children would be unclean, but now they are holy. (I Corinthians 7:14)

[...] to the weak I became as weak, that I might win the weak. I have become all things to all *men*, that I might by all means save some. (I Corinthians 9:22)

And now abide faith, hope, love, these three; but the greatest of these *is* love. (I Corinthians 13:13)

[...] and that He was buried, and that He rose again the third day according to the Scriptures, and that He was seen by Cephas, then by the twelve. After that He was seen by over five hundred brethren at once, of whom the greater part remain to the present, but some have fallen asleep. (I Corinthians 15:4-6)

Awake to righteousness, and do not sin; for some do not have the knowledge of God. I speak *this* to your shame.
(I Corinthians 15:34)

For we are to God the fragrance of Christ among those who are being saved and among those who are perishing. To the one *we are* the aroma of death *leading* to death, and to the other the aroma of life *leading* to life. And who *is* sufficient for these things?
(II Corinthians 2:15, 16)

You are our epistle written in our hearts, known and read by all men; (II Corinthians 3:2)

For it is the God who commanded light to shine out of darkness, who has shone in our hearts to *give* the light of the knowledge of the glory of God in the face of Jesus Christ.
(II Corinthians 4:6)

For we must all appear before the judgment seat of Christ, that each one may receive the things *done* in the body, according to what he has done, whether good or bad. Knowing, therefore, the terror of the Lord, we persuade men; but we are well known to God, and I also trust are well known in your consciences.
(II Corinthians 5:10, 11)

For the love of Christ compels us, because we judge thus: that if One died for all, then all died; (II Corinthians 5:14)

Now all things *are* of God, who has reconciled us to Himself through Jesus Christ, and has given us the ministry of reconciliation, [...] Now then, we are ambassadors for Christ, as though God were pleading through us: we implore *you* on Christ's behalf, be reconciled to God. (II Corinthians 5:18, 20)

For He says:
"In an acceptable time I have heard you,
And in the day of salvation I have helped you."
Behold, now *is* the accepted time; behold, now *is* the day of salvation. (II Corinthians 6:2)

For godly sorrow produces repentance *leading* to salvation, not to be regretted; but the sorrow of the world produces death. (II Corinthians 7:10)

[...] to preach the gospel in the *regions* beyond you, *and* not to boast in another man's sphere of accomplishment. But *"he who glories, let him glory in the* LORD.*"* (II Corinthians 10:16, 17)

[...] to reveal His Son in me, that I might preach Him among the Gentiles, I did not immediately confer with flesh and blood, (Galatians 1:16)

"knowing that a man is not justified by the works of the law but by faith in Jesus Christ, even we have believed in Christ Jesus, that we might be justified by faith in Christ and not by the works of the law; for by the works of the law no flesh shall be justified. For I through the law died to the law that I might live to God. (Galatians 2:16, 19)

[...] just as Abraham *"believed God, and it was accounted to him for righteousness."* Therefore know that *only* those who are of faith are sons of Abraham. And the Scripture, foreseeing that God would justify the Gentiles by faith, preached the gospel to Abraham beforehand, *saying, "In you all the nations shall be blessed."* So then those who are of faith are blessed with believing Abraham. Christ has redeemed us from the curse of the law, having become a curse for us (for it is written, *"Cursed is everyone who hangs on a tree"*), that the blessing of Abraham might come upon the Gentiles in Christ Jesus, that we might receive the promise of the Spirit through faith. (Galatians 3:6-9, 13, 14)

For by grace you have been saved through faith, and that not of yourselves; *it is* the gift of God, not of works, lest anyone should boast. (Ephesians 2:8, 9)

And He Himself gave some *to be* apostles, some prophets, some evangelists, and some pastors and teachers, for the equipping of the saints for the work of ministry, for the edifying of the body of Christ, (Ephesians 4:11, 12)

[...] and having shod your feet with the preparation of the gospel of peace; (Ephesians 6:15)

[...] that at the name of Jesus every knee should bow, of those in heaven, and of those on earth, and of those under the earth, and *that* every tongue should confess that Jesus Christ *is* Lord, to the glory of God the Father. (Philippians 2:10, 11)

Do all things without complaining and disputing, that you may become blameless and harmless, children of God without fault in the midst of a crooked and perverse generation, among whom you shine as lights in the world, holding fast the word of life, so that I may rejoice in the day of Christ that I have not run in vain or labored in vain. (Philippians 2:14-16)

Him we preach, warning every man and teaching every man in all wisdom, that we may present every man perfect in Christ Jesus. To this *end* I also labor, striving according to His working which works in me mightily. (Colossians 1:28, 29)

[...] meanwhile praying also for us, that God would open to us a door for the word, to speak the mystery of Christ, for which I am also in chains, that I may make it manifest, as I ought to speak. Walk in wisdom toward those *who are* outside, redeeming the time. *Let* your speech always *be* with grace, seasoned with salt, that you may know how you ought to answer each one. (Colossians 4:3-6)

For what *is* our hope, or joy, or crown of rejoicing? *Is it* not even you in the presence of our Lord Jesus Christ at His coming? For you are our glory and joy. (I Thessalonians 2:19, 20)

For the Lord Himself will descend from heaven with a shout, with the voice of an archangel, and with the trumpet of God. And the dead in Christ will rise first. Then we who are alive and remain shall be caught up together with them in the clouds to meet the Lord in the air. And thus we shall always be with the Lord. (I Thessalonians 4:16, 17)

And I thank Christ Jesus our Lord who has enabled me, because He counted me faithful, putting *me* into the ministry, (I Timothy 1:12)

This *is* a faithful saying and worthy of all acceptance, that Christ Jesus came into the world to save sinners, of whom I am chief. (I Timothy 1:15)

For this *is* good and acceptable in the sight of God our Savior, who desires all men to be saved and to come to the knowledge of the truth. For *there is* one God and one Mediator between God and men, *the* Man Christ Jesus, (I Timothy 2:3-5)

And the things that you have heard from me among many witnesses, commit these to faithful men who will be able to teach others also. (II Timothy 2:2)

[...] in humility correcting those who are in opposition, if God perhaps will grant them repentance, so that they may know the truth, and *that* they may come to their senses *and escape* the snare of the devil, having been taken captive by him to do his will. (II Timothy 2:25, 26)

But you be watchful in all things, endure afflictions, do the work of an evangelist, fulfill your ministry. (II Timothy 4:5)

But the Lord stood with me and strengthened me, so that the message might be preached fully through me, and *that* all the Gentiles might hear. Also I was delivered out of the mouth of the lion. (II Timothy 4:17)

For the grace of God that brings salvation has appeared to all men, teaching us that, denying ungodliness and worldly lusts, we should live soberly, righteously, and godly in the present age, looking for the blessed hope and glorious appearing of our great God and Savior Jesus Christ, who gave Himself for us, that He might redeem us from every lawless deed and purify for Himself *His* own special people, zealous for good works. (Titus 2:11-14)

[...] not by works of righteousness which we have done, but according to His mercy He saved us, through the washing of regeneration and renewing of the Holy Spirit, that having been justified by His grace we should become heirs according to the hope of eternal life. (Titus 3:5, 7)

[...] that the sharing of your faith may become effective by the acknowledgment of every good thing which is in you in Christ Jesus. (Philemon 1:6)

Therefore He is also able to save to the uttermost those who come to God through Him, since He always lives to make intercession for them. (Hebrews 7:25)

"For I will be merciful to their unrighteousness, and their sins and their lawless deeds I will remember no more."
(Hebrews 8:12)

For if the blood of bulls and goats and the ashes of a heifer, sprinkling the unclean, sanctifies for the purifying of the flesh, how much more shall the blood of Christ, who through the eternal Spirit offered Himself without spot to God, cleanse your conscience from dead works to serve the living God? And for this reason He is the Mediator of the new covenant, by means of death, for the redemption of the transgressions under the first covenant, that those who are called may receive the promise of the eternal inheritance. (Hebrews 9:13-15)

By faith Noah, being divinely warned of things not yet seen, moved with godly fear, prepared an ark for the saving of his household, by which he condemned the world and became heir of the righteousness which is according to faith.
(Hebrews 11:7)

Brethren, if anyone among you wanders from the truth, and someone turns him back, let him know that he who turns a sinner from the error of his way will save a soul from death and cover a multitude of sins. (James 5:19, 20)

Therefore it is also contained in the Scripture,
"Behold, I lay in Zion
A chief cornerstone, elect, precious,
And he who believes on Him will by no means be put to shame."
(I Peter 2:6)

Therefore, brethren, be even more diligent to make your call and election sure, for if you do these things you will never stumble; for so an entrance will be supplied to you abundantly into the everlasting kingdom of our Lord and Savior Jesus Christ. (II Peter 1:10, 11)

The Lord is not slack concerning *His* promise, as some count Slackness, but is longsuffering toward us, not willing that any should perish but that all should come to repentance. (II Peter 3:9)

Therefore, since all these things will be dissolved, what manner *of persons* ought you to be in holy conduct and godliness, looking for and hastening the coming of the day of God, because of which the heavens will be dissolved, being on fire, and the elements will melt with fervent heat? (II Peter 3:11, 12)

This is the message which we have heard from Him and declare to you, that God is light and in Him is no darkness at all. But if we walk in the light as He is in the light, we have fellowship with one another, and the blood of Jesus Christ His Son cleanses us from all sin. (I John 1:5, 7)

And this is the promise that He has promised us—eternal life. (I John 2:25)

And this is the testimony: that God has given us eternal life, and this life is in His Son. He who has the Son has life; he who does not have the Son of God does not have life. These things I have written to you who believe in the name of the Son of God, that you may know that you have eternal life, and that you may *continue to* believe in the name of the Son of God. (I John 5:11-13)

And on some have compassion, making a distinction; but others save with fear, pulling *them* out of the fire, hating even the garment defiled by the flesh. (Jude 1:22, 23)

Behold, He is coming with clouds, and every eye will see Him, even they who pierced Him. And all the tribes of the earth will mourn because of Him. Even so, Amen. "I am the Alpha and the Omega, *the* Beginning and *the* End," says the Lord, "who is and who was and who is to come, the Almighty." (Revelation 1:7, 8)

Nevertheless I have *this* against you, that you have left your first love. Remember therefore from where you have fallen; repent and do the first works, or else I will come to you quickly and remove your lampstand from its place—unless you repent. (Revelation 2:4, 5)

"Because you say, 'I am rich, have become wealthy, and have need of nothing'—and do not know that you are wretched, miserable, poor, blind, and naked— "I counsel you to buy from Me gold refined in the fire, that you may be rich; and white garments, that you may be clothed, *that* the shame of your nakedness may not be revealed; and anoint your eyes with eye salve, that you may see.

"As many as I love, I rebuke and chasten. Therefore be zealous and repent. "Behold, I stand at the door and knock. If anyone hears My voice and opens the door, I will come in to him and dine with him, and he with Me. (Revelation 3:17-20)

Then I looked, and I heard the voice of many angels around the throne, the living creatures, and the elders; and the number of them was ten thousand times ten thousand, and thousands of thousands, saying with a loud voice:
"Worthy is the Lamb who was slain
To receive power and riches and wisdom,
And strength and honor and glory and blessing!"
And every creature which is in heaven and on the earth and under the earth and such as are in the sea, and all that are in them, I heard saying: "Blessing and honor and glory and power
Be to Him who sits on the throne,
And to the Lamb, forever and ever!"
(Revelation 5:11-13)

After these things I looked, and behold, a great multitude which no one could number, of all nations, tribes, peoples, and tongues, standing before the throne and before the Lamb, clothed with white robes, with palm branches in their hands, and crying out with a loud voice, saying, "Salvation *belongs* to our God who sits on the throne, and to the Lamb!" (Revelation 7:9, 10)

And they overcame him by the blood of the Lamb and by the word of their testimony, and they did not love their lives to the death. (Revelation 12:11)

Then I saw another angel flying in the midst of heaven, having the everlasting gospel to preach to those who dwell on the earth—to every nation, tribe, tongue, and people—saying with a loud voice,

"Fear God and give glory to Him, for the hour of His judgment has come; and worship Him who made heaven and earth, the sea and springs of water." (Revelation 14:6, 7)

And I fell at his feet to worship him. But he said to me, "See *that you do* not *do that!* I am your fellow servant, and of your brethren who have the testimony of Jesus. Worship God! For the testimony of Jesus is the spirit of prophecy." (Revelation 19:10)

"And behold, I am coming quickly, and My reward *is* with Me, to give to every one according to his work.
(Revelation 22:12)

"Behold, I am coming quickly! Blessed *is* he who keeps the words of the prophecy of this book." He who testifies to these things says, "Surely I am coming quickly." Amen. Even so, come, Lord Jesus!
(Revelation 22:7, 20)